Ruth Vouras

8-8-75

Western Yr. Mtg. Friends

(Supply swap)

Conscience
and
Liberty

By the Same Author

AN A B C OF WAR TIME LAW
(Hamish Hamilton, 1s.; Legal Edition, 2s. 6d.)

AFTER THE RAID IS OVER
(Hamish Hamilton, 6d.)

TIME TO PAY
(Hamish Hamilton, 6d.)

Conscience

and

Liberty

by
ROBERT S. W. POLLARD

London
George Allen and Unwin Ltd

FIRST PUBLISHED IN 1940

PRINTED IN GREAT BRITAIN
in 10-Point Plantin Type
BY UNWIN BROTHERS LIMITED
WOKING

Foreword

This short essay is an attempt to show how the question of freedom of conscience cannot be separated from liberty of opinion. It was necessary to present a clear conception of what conscience is before restating the case for freedom. It has not been possible to deal with freedom in every department and every aspect of the individual life. I would, however, like to acknowledge here my debt to the Promethean Society and the Federation of Progressive Societies and Individuals (now the Progressive League) who did much to bring out the need for free opinion and action in these spheres of life. Liberty is too often thought of as concerned only with politics and economics. To maintain liberty and democracy in the collectivized state which is now inevitable will demand a firm grasp of principle. I hope that this essay will help to promote this understanding of the necessity of liberty in any good society. A knowledge of principle and of the struggle for liberty will encourage us to resist the onslaughts now being made upon it, and make its resurgence more sure.

I should like to acknowledge here my debt to my wife, Beatrice E. Pollard, without whose aid this essay would never have been written. I am also most grateful to my father, Francis E. Pollard, and Mr. James Avery Joyce of the Inner Temple for their kindness in reading the manuscript and making suggestions.

My thanks are also due to the authors and publishers for permission to quote from the following books: *Why We Do Right*, by C. T. Gorham (Watts & Co.); *Liberty Today*, by Dr. C. E. M. Joad (Watts & Co.); *Liberty in the Modern State*, by Professor Harold J. Laski (Faber & Faber, Ltd.); *A History of Freedom of Thought*, by J. B. Bury (Thornton Butterworth, Ltd.); *Historical Trials*, by Sir John MacDonell (Clarendon Press, Oxford); *The Quakers in Peace and War*, by Margaret E. Hirst (George Allen &

Unwin); *Penalties Upon Opinion*, by H. P. Bonner (Thinker's Library, Watts & Co.); *Conscription and Conscience*, by J. W. Graham (George Allen & Unwin); *After the Deluge*, by Leonard Woolf (The Hogarth Press); *Dictatorship*, by Alfred Cobban (Jonathan Cape, Ltd.); *Democracy Up to Date*, by Sir Stafford Cripps (George Allen & Unwin); *A History of European Liberalism*, by G. de Ruggiero (Clarendon Press, Oxford); *The New Despotism*, by Lord Hewart (Ernest Benn, Ltd.).

Contents

FOREWORD   PAGE 7

CHAPTER

1. WHAT IS CONSCIENCE?   11

2. FIRST PRINCIPLES OF LIBERTY   20

3. A SURVEY OF PERSECUTION   31

4. LIBERTY IN CHAINS, 1914–1918   51

5. BETWEEN TWO WARS   69

6. THE GROWTH OF BUREAUCRACY   75

7. FREEDOM NOW   83

8. MILITARY CONSCRIPTION   95

9. WHAT OF THE FUTURE?   104

Suggestions for further Reading   119

INDEX   121

CONTENTS

FOREWORD

CHAPTER

1. WHAT IS CONSCIENCE? 13

2. RIGHT PRINCIPLES OF CHOICE 29

3. TESTS OF PERFECTION 42

4. CERTAIN IN CHANGE, 1914–1918 51

5. BETWEEN TWO WARS 63

6. THE GROWTH OF DEMOCRACY 77

7. FREEDOM NOW 87

8. MILITARY CONSCRIPTION 95

9. WHAT OF THE FUTURE? 104

Suggestions for Further Reading 110

Chapter 1

WHAT IS CONSCIENCE?

How many other things might be tolerated in peace and left to conscience, had we but charity, and were it not the chief stronghold of our hypocrisy to be ever judging one another.

MILTON (*Areopagitica*)

What is conscience? And what is its relation to liberty and therefore to law and the State?

The earliest recognition of conscience in English law was in the middle ages, when a system of law now known as Equity developed to mitigate the harshness of the common law. Equity was sometimes known as Conscience, and the Court of Equity (the Court of Chancery) was sometimes known as a Court of Conscience or a Court where justice would be done irrespective of the rules of the common law.

The Conscription Acts during the 1914–18 war and the present war have provided that those whose consciences were against taking part in warfare should have some form of exemption, if a tribunal were satisfied that their consciences were genuine. The Vaccination Acts of 1898 and 1907 provide that any parent who conscientiously objects to the compulsory vaccination of his children can avoid having this done on making a statutory declaration. Nowhere, however, is there any definition of conscience.

English law then, in several places, recognizes this phenomenon. But what is it in its nature and significance? Many are the explanations offered. These roughly fall into two groups: the religious, which sees conscience as a divinely implanted faculty and therefore distinct from and inevitably other than human mental activity; and the biological, which regards conscience as one of the *functions* of the human mind, fundamentally no different from other mental phenomena. It is true that these two views may be as it were combined, if you regard the natural activities of the spirit of man as implying some divine endowment. But for the purposes we have in mind, this essay will adopt the second view and for three reasons. First, the view that sees conscience as a special divine intervention in the composition of the human mind is open to objection, on the ground that it is an unnecessarily elaborate and *ad hoc* explanation which increases difficulty when dealing with the manifestations of conscience. It purports to explain conscience without in fact explaining it at all. Further, this view of conscience seems to hark back to that old "faculty psychology" against which a great weight of experimental evidence has been accumulated.

Secondly, in the name of conscience, millions have been slaughtered and tortured and every kind of moral iniquity has been practised. To make conscience dependent on God in any way that takes no account of man's responsibility and fallibility is to depreciate that on which it is dependent. Conscience leads to a variety of acts: one man's conscience will lead him to take part in war, another to abstain. The voice of conscience is frequently ineffective. This variety and ineffectiveness would reflect on God if He were responsible.

Thirdly, the functional conception of conscience is compatible with the findings of at least some of the chief schools of psychological thought. To the others the whole subject of conscience might be said to be at present irrelevant. This is largely because they are concerned to develop experimental techniques rather than offer generalizations. They do not deny the existence of conscience, nor that relation to the mind which is suggested above. Their scope has simply not been extended to cover it. We may therefore tentatively conclude that psychology raises no objection to the functional view of conscience.

Mr. C. T. Gorham expresses this view with great clarity in his valuable book *Why We Do Right*[1]: "The limitations of language compel us to speak of mental functions as if each were a separate power complete in itself, having a definite province and definite limits, yet acting harmoniously with other powers. But in allotting a special area to each function we are really indicating one mode in which the mind works."

F. Hislop in his article on conscience in the *Encyclopaedia of Religion and Ethics* states that conscience has three elements: (1) Cognitive, (2) emotional, (3) desiderative or conative. In other words conscience like any other mental activity comprises an intellectual factor, a factor of feeling and a factor of striving. But we are particularly concerned to emphasize the intellectual or reasoning element.

It is obvious that there is no code of fixed and standard rules to which conscience can automatically refer or by which the moral sense can mechanically pronounce judgment. Conscience will for example say theft is wrong, but who will say that the case of an unemployed man who takes a loaf of bread for his starving family is not on a different plane from that of the man who embezzles money in order to live on the Riviera?

It is true that moral judgments may be arrived at so quickly that they seem to be instinctive and intuitive. A man who has been brought up a pacifist and whose friends and relations have been mainly pacifist may well say, if faced with joining the army, that he feels that it is instinctively against his nature and contrary to his conscience. Such a horrified aversion may have always been, without exception, his reaction to any situation of physical conflict. Generally it has been accepted from his parents or others and no other reaction has at any time seemed natural to him. It has not been built up by a process of thought and could be broken down only with extreme difficulty. As he nears maturity, taking thought rather adds outer bulwarks of defence to his position. On the other hand, a conscientious objection to war may be in large part the work of conscious experience and thought.

[1] Watts & Co., 1924.

When firmly established, however, its manifestations in moral judgments can occur with all the speed of habitual reactions. A highly developed and sensitive conscience dispenses, in certain situations, with the delays both of long pondered judgments and of emotional conflict.

It is sometimes considered that the essence of conscience is to be found in the sense of shame and remorse. What is to be said of this position? One or two points at least may be noted. Feelings of grief at moral failure do not develop in any case except at a later and complex stage of individual or communal development. Psycho-analysts, however, maintain that these are feelings engendered, in the first place, by the conflicts set up in the infant mind by the over-zealous attempts of mother or nurse to exact civilized restraint in the child's physical habits. Subsequently, it is suggested, any discrepancy between conduct and the ideal, perhaps unwillingly accepted, tends to evoke similar distress of mind. Significantly enough, any close observer may note that as acceptance of an ideal becomes fuller and more real, the remorse felt, when actual conduct "misses the mark," does not necessarily become more painful. This would suggest that some of what passes as "shame" or "remorse" is not entirely healthy or desirable; it can hardly be essential at any rate. From this slight sketch of the mental elements which conscience is thought to comprise, we turn to the processes of its development in the individual and in the community.

Intelligence develops differently and attains various levels, and it is its co-ordination and adjustment with feeling and striving that partially explain the varieties of conscientious action. It is during this process of interaction that education has its part to play, as well as in the exercise of the most delicate discretion during the imposition of the earliest restraints upon the child.

In some savage tribes young men were, until recently, expected to commit murders as a proof of prowess, and in some cases public opinion would applaud a man who committed the greatest number: but education of the individual has removed this idea from the minds of the so-called civilized peoples. Individual murder is universally recognized as wrong: the mass slaughter of individuals in warfare, however, is still regarded as morally right by the majority, and not until they and their statesmen regard it as morally wrong will it cease.

It is interesting to speculate as to what attitude would be taken by the majority to an Englishman who had a private feud with a German officer and who murdered this officer during this war on coming across him in a neutral country. It is probable that some of the majority would condemn the act and if an Englishman murdered a German prisoner of war in England, his act would be condemned by more. He would no doubt be brought to trial for murder, but it is unlikely that he would be hanged. It is evident then that human actions with their bewildering variety of motive and circumstance, require that the judging mind—for itself or upon others—should be capable of nice distinctions.

This is not the place to go in much detail into the questions of the origin of conscience. We must, however, conclude that, for the reasons given earlier in this chapter, it evolved from simpler mental elements, and can be observed in various stages of its evolution in persons all around us to-day. Its effects on the conduct of some are spasmodic, on that of others steady and dominating. Moreover, it seems to be closely associated with those persistent tendencies towards self-integration which appear to mark the healthy developing personality.

Anthropological studies suggest that the primitive conscience was not individual but wholly a function of the tribal group. The growth of self-consciousness lifted the individual out of that undistinguished situation. Yet the community has never wholly lost its power, exercised directly or indirectly, over the individual conscience. It is, of course, strictly inconceivable that it should do so. However, it would appear that the future of conscience lies in the widening of the conception of the community to which the individual conscience is organically bound. Not the tribe or the nation; can we think of it as humanity? And, reciprocally, if the development of conscience is to be both complete and effective, the several communities will have, in fact, to widen (i.e. unite) themselves, in some measure, at least, in order to bring the appropriate educative influence to bear on the individual. Conscience, like self-consciousness, appears first of all as a group phenomenon, then centralized in the individual, and in its third stage it becomes, or should become, an harmonization of the individual conscience and the moral judgments of the community.

Conscience in the individual is, therefore, a product of the previous experience of the race operating as part of his environment, and his own reaction to this, more or less modified by reason.

Particularly important in the development of the individual modern conscience is the parental and school influence of the first few years of life. This may well determine the development and expression of the individual's conscience, for this is intimately related to—if not ultimately based on—sympathy. Sir Leslie Stephen says: "Sympathy is not an additional instinct, a faculty which is added when the mind has reached a certain stage of development, a mere incident of intellectual growth, but something implied from the first in the very structure of knowledge. . . . 'Put yourself in his place,' is not merely a moral precept; it is a logical rule implied in the earliest germs of reason as a description of reasoning itself, so far as it deals with other sentient beings. To know that a man has certain feelings is to have representative feelings, not equal in intensity, but identical in kind. Sympathy and reason have so far an identical factor—each implies the other. . . . The two processes are mutually involved, and, whatever difficulties may be suggested, it seems clear that I cannot properly know what another man feels without in some degree feeling what he feels."[1]

The view of conscience put forward by Hislop and also by

[1] *Science of Ethics*, p. 230.

16

Gorham is neatly summarized by the latter as follows: "It is thus evident that conscience is a function of the mind which examines and pronounces upon the relations of human beings to one another. The emotional side is made up of love (or sympathy, which is a form of love) and fear of the disapproval of others; the intellectual part is the perception of the rightness or wrongness of the social adjustment. This mingling of the emotional desires with intellectual determination has, through long experience, evolved conscience." Conscience is, therefore, a judgment of the whole integrated personality upon some moral or ethical issue.

What is the authority of conscience? The problem may be discussed from various points of view. We may ask what is the origin or explanation of the fact that conscience speaks with authority, or again whether its pronouncements are beyond question.

It has been suggested that the idea of "ought" is derived from primitive notions of economic justice formed by the interchange of goods and services.[1] The word itself is derived from the same word root as the word "owe" relating to a debt, and thus embodies the idea of justice, which is developed with the growth of society. But this view would not appear to take into account sufficiently the emotional and biological factors involved.

Further discussion as to the origin of the imperativeness of the moral sense cannot be dealt with here. Nor do I propose to to voice any opinion as to what the good is which man pursues, although this problem is intimately connected with that of conscience. Lowes Dickinson in *The Meaning of Good* suggests that in our relation to other persons in the form of love there is something that comes nearest to the experience of absolute good.

In any case the fact remains that it is of the essence of conscience that it does speak with authority, and no theory as to its evolution can alter this.

But that conscience is infallible is another matter altogether.

[1] See C. T. Gorham, p. 53.

There is a sense in which all thinking carries with it a claim to speak with authority. But as thought may be wrong, so conscience may be wrong. However strong the feeling that conscience commands a particular action may be, the feeling in itself adds nothing to the validity of the moral judgment.

It is a question of the degree of enlightenment of the particular conscience. The person who regards it as immoral for games to be played on Sundays has an "ignorant conscience," while the conscience which sees immorality in poverty, war and unemployment is considerably more enlightened. Members of the Inquisition who condemned heretics to be burnt felt very strongly that this was in conformity with their consciences. This did not make their judgment valid. Feelings of obligation can be derived from emotions often very inconsistent with each other and little modified by reason.

We have now reached the position that the verdict of conscience may not always be right. If consciences are the product of mental and environmental conditions their orders will vary according to these. A person must not blindly obey the first dictate which appears to be formulated by conscience. He must reason and enquire into it and establish if it is sound. Conscience is and must be modified and altered by a growth of knowledge and intelligence. Behind conscience stands the experience of the community. This is generally accepted as a guide because it is in the individual's true interest to accept it, and the more he is adjusted and harmonized to the best life in the community, often the more truly happy he is, but the authority and the experience of the community is not final. The ultimate authority of conscience is found in the individual, who must endeavour to review the problem from every angle, to think through its implications to the utmost of his ability, and then, without fear of popular prejudice or dogma or authority, "having done all" must reach and stand by his own decision. Whether this conflicts with the immediate judgment of the community or not, it should be respected and the individual's conscience should be left free, for, given these conditions, such a judgment will be in harmony with and not against the highest good of the community.

One other matter may be referred to. It has been stated by tribunals under the National Service (Armed Forces) Act that a political objection to war cannnot be conscientious. This phrase may be described as "potted thinking." What is really meant is that a man who objects to a particular war and all the evils it gives rise to is not a conscientious objector if he might, under quite different circumstances, not object to some other war. It will be obvious, however, from what has been said, that if such moral decision is arrived at in the manner described above it is as valid and should be as much respected as any other decision of conscience. A particular war may be as immoral and wrong to a Socialist as to a Christian. Behind this suggestion lies the contemporary assumption that morals are irrelevant to politics. The present state of the world, in part at least a result of this assumption, should at least suggest a doubt as to its wisdom.

Chapter 2

FIRST PRINCIPLES OF LIBERTY

Thy birthplace—where, young Liberty?
In graves, 'mid heroes' ashes.
Thy dwelling—where, sweet Liberty?
In hearts, where free blood dashes.

Thy safety—where, stray Liberty?
In lands where discord cease.
Thy glory—where, bright Liberty?
In Universal Peace.

ERNEST JONES, *Chartist Poet*

Liberty is most easily preserved when the principles which lie behind it are understood and absorbed, and here an attempt will be made to remind the reader of the basis upon which liberty of opinion depends. The expression "liberty of opinion" is here used to include liberty of speech and writing, and liberty to combine to express opinions in action, i.e. the freedom to meet together and to form societies, trade unions, churches and parties for political, religious, industrial and social purposes.

The case for freedom was so cogently enunciated by John Stuart Mill in his essay *On Liberty*[1] that it would be presumptuous on the author's part to attempt to do anything but recapitulate his leading points. Unfortunately few practical politicians and persons engaged in the administration of the country appear to read Mill.

If Liberty is to be secure it must be understood, and understood as something more than a vague emotional catchword.

[1] Thinker's Library, 1s. 3d.

Such a book as Susan Stebbing's *Thinking to Some Purpose*[1] is of great assistance in clarifying the mind in its reaction to slogans and popular assumptions, and more particularly in sifting the significant from the meaningless.

Let us see how Mill can help. He puts the case for freedom of opinion on four grounds, which may be summarized as follows:—

(1) Opinion which is suppressed—whether by governments or majorities—may very likely be true. To deny this is to assume that governments or majorities are infallible. The suppression of opinions and experiments in living will mean the suppression of truth and the prevention of improvements to a greater or less degree.

(2) Even if the suppressed opinion is untrue it may, and generally does, contain some truth. Since the prevailing opinion on any subject is never wholly true, it is only by the clash of conflicting opinions that the remainder of the truth in question has any chance of coming to light. This is the only way to keep truth fresh in men's minds and vital to influence their motives and conduct. New truth is in a minority of one when first thought of, and it has to struggle through oppression and obloquy to make its way. To meet by force that which should be met only by argument and persuasion is to put humanity in permanent danger of losing sources of enlightenment and progress.

(3) If the prevailing opinion contained the whole truth it would by most people be held as a dogma without being understood, unless it was allowed to be, and actually was, vigorously and earnestly contested. To hold an opinion as a dogma prevents the growth of character and conviction for which an atmosphere of freedom is essential.

(4) If the prevailing opinion is not allowed to be contested, its inmost meaning will be in danger of being lost or enfeebled, to become a mere dogma, useless for good. So the better means

[1] Pelican Books, 6d.

of influencing men, such as education, will be discredited and frustrated. Moreover, it is better that men should differ and each lead his own life, developing his faculties in his own way, and make the most of himself by his own efforts, than that all should be drilled into a mechanical perfection.

The neglect of these principles led to the condemnation of Socrates and to innumerable other persecutions, some of which are dealt with in the succeeding pages.

It cannot be too often repeated that there is the greatest difference between presuming an opinion to be true, because with every opportunity for arguing against it it has not been proved wrong (e.g. any scientific law), and assuming its truth for the purpose of not allowing it to be refuted or argued against (e.g. the prohibition of anti-war literature in time of war).

It is important in these days to remember Mill's exposure of the fallacy that persecution does truth good. He said: "The dictum that truth always triumphs over persecution is one of those pleasant falsehoods which men repeat after one another till they pass into commonplaces, but which all experience refutes. History teems with instances of truth put down by persecution. If not suppressed for ever, it may be thrown back for centuries. To speak only of religious opinions: the Reformation broke out at least twenty times before Luther, and was put down. Arnold of Brescia was put down. Fra Dolcino was put down. Savonarola was put down. The Albigeois were put down. The Vaudois were put down. The Lollards were put down. The Hussites were put down. Even after the era of Luther, wherever persecution was persisted in, it was successful. In Spain, Italy, Flanders, the Austrian Empire, Protestantism was rooted out; and most likely would have been so in England had Queen Mary lived or Queen Elizabeth died. Persecution has always succeeded, save where the heretics were too strong a party to be effectually persecuted. No reasonable person can doubt that Christianity might have been extirpated in the Roman Empire. It spread, and became predominant, because the persecutions were only occasional, lasting but a short time and separated by long intervals of almost undisturbed propagandism. It is a piece of idle sentimentality that truth, merely as truth, has any inherent power, denied to error, of prevailing against the dungeon and the stake. Men are not more zealous for truth than they often are for error, and a sufficient application of legal or even of social penalties will generally succeed in stopping the propagation of either. The real advantage which truth has consists in this, that when an opinion is true it may be extinguished once, twice or many times, but in the course of ages there will generally be found persons to rediscover it, until some one of its reappearances falls on a time when from favourable circumstances it escapes persecution until it has made such head as to withstand all subsequent attempts to suppress it."

It is sometimes argued that freedom of opinion may be permitted but should only be expressed in certain ways, e.g. in moderate language. A man, it is suggested, may rightly be prosecuted for words which seem likely to provoke a breach of the peace. But this is a real repression of opinion. Words which to one magistrate are not insulting will seem grossly so to another. The test should be whether a breach of the peace has actually taken place, when the matter passes from freedom of expression of opinion to that of a crime for which society may rightly exact a penalty.

Mill continues his exposition by laying it down that men must be free to act on their opinions, otherwise freedom of opinion is of little value. The only limitation must be that the individual must not make himself a nuisance to other people. . . . If a man avoids hurting others in what concerns them, and merely acts according to his own judgment in things which concern himself, the same reasons which show that opinion should be free prove also that he should be allowed, without molestation, to carry his opinions into action at his own risk.

"That mankind are not infallible; that their truths for the

23

most part are only half-truths; that unity of opinion, unless resulting from the fullest and freest comparison of opposite opinions, is not desirable, and diversity not an evil, but a good, until mankind are much more capable than at present of recognizing all sides of the truth, are principles applicable to men's modes of action, not less than to their opinions. As it is useful that while mankind are imperfect there should be different opinions, so it is that there should be different experiments of living; that free scope should be given to varieties of character, short of injury to others; and that the worth of different modes of life should be proved practically, when anyone thinks fit to try them. It is desirable, in short, that in things which do not primarily concern others individuality should assert itself. Where, not the person's own character, but the traditions or customs of other people, are the rule of conduct, there is wanting one of the principal ingredients of human happiness and quite the chief ingredient of individual and social progress."

This challenge to the freedom of the individual in action comes not only from the State but from the coercive effect of public opinion; the demands of custom, convention and formality tend to press the individual into a common pattern. This tendency, which Mill pointed out, is much accentuated to-day by the mass standardization of public opinion by means of modern newspapers, the B.B.C., the cinema and the State education system. These institutions, which are largely the product of the present economic system, will remain dangerous until the libertarian principles here insisted upon are universally taught, accepted and acted upon.

Moreover, if the purpose of the State is to promote the welfare and happiness of its members, it is essential that the individual must be free to choose for himself his own kind of life and what he should do with it. Liberty is essential for the complete development of personality. In so far as the State passes obscenity laws, blasphemy laws and sedition laws and censors films and plays, it assumes that it is infallible about certain aspects of truth and morality and so far does it crush the personalities of its citizens.

A State has to maintain—and it is indeed its duty—certain standards and rules of behaviour, so that liberty is possible to all, and so that the individual's personality may be properly developed. It is easy enough to show that, for example, neither the rules requiring traffic to keep to the left-hand side of the road nor the compulsory education of children are an invasion of these principles of true liberty.

To suppress opinions on the ground that they are false is to suppose that the opposing doctrine is true. Yet this is very rarely the case. Beliefs about religion and the physical world have been implicitly accepted in one era and completely rejected in another. Such are, for example, the story that the world was created in seven days and the beliefs in alchemy. These concepts, now disregarded by all intelligent men, were once as widely accepted as the current theory of the internal combustion engine. If there had been a State educational system in the Middle Ages, no doubt alchemy and the creation of the world would have been taught as true in the same way as nowadays in England the belief in the benefit that the British Empire bestows upon the world is inculcated, or in Germany Nazi myths about Nordic men and German racial superiority, or in Russia the perfection of Stalin and his rule and system, become tacit assumptions among the young. Many of these current prejudices, beliefs and dogmas can either be proved to be false or, at any rate, cannot be proved to be true. Yet suppression of the opposite opinions assumes that the current and prevailing view is true and has an inherent right to suppress all others.

In a famous passage on the need for scepticism, Bertrand Russell (quoted by Dr. C. E. M. Joad in *Liberty To-day*) divides beliefs into those held by experts and those held by non-experts. After pointing out that even the belief of experts does not make an opinion certain, he ventures the view that it is, nevertheless, more likely to be right than that of non-experts. He then proceeds to enunciate the following three propositions as embodying the basis of a reasonable scepticism:—

"(1) That when the experts are agreed, the opposite opinion cannot be held to be certain; (2) that when they are not agreed, no opinion can be regarded as certain by a non-expert; and (3) that when they all hold that no sufficient grounds for a positive opinion exist, the ordinary man would do well to suspend his judgment."

What control is the State entitled to exercise over parties, churches, trade unions, societies and bodies who have joined together for action in some field in which they have a common interest, and this even if their opinions are disputable?

The internal life and affairs of societies should not be interfered with at all. It is only where their opinions and practices go outside this field that interference may be justified. A society of nudists should be as free to practise and advocate nudity as a monastery of monks or church is free to practise and advocate celibacy. Moreover, these associations must be free to decide their sphere of activity. It is not for authority to prevent a trade union undertaking political activity or a community centre discussing foreign affairs. Interference by the State with such bodies as churches and trade unions has, in the past, led time after time to conflict. What is even more serious, however, voluntary associations with their vitality and spontaneity are the natural flowering of the vigour of a democratic State, and to tamper with them is to dry them up at the source.

It is impossible to deny the State the right to suppress organizations which exist to overthrow it by force and not by peaceful means, for the State must assume that it is itself worth preserving. But this right does not entitle a Government to suppress societies on the ground that their beliefs if crystallized in action would be subversive to the State. For to do this would be to persecute people merely for holding opinions. It is only when action designed to overthrow the State is actually taking place, that intervention can properly be justified. If, for instance, a body of men commence military drill or collect arms and ammunition, then they can properly be suppressed. Unless the commission of some overt act such as organizing activities likely to be useful to an enemy is made essential before a body can be interfered with (as Laski says in his *Liberty in the Modern State*) a Government will be able to attack an organization merely because it dislikes its views. This would put the whole of liberty of opinion and freedom of conscience in danger. The modern State, which claims this right, has in fact put both liberty and conscience in danger as we shall see.

Moreover, it must be remembered that force is never a reply to argument—although it is often assumed to be—and that the persecution of opinion grows by what it feeds on. Once allow suppression to begin, and all the fanatics who wish to suppress people who dissent from their views will seize the chance to make this dissent a crime.

Voluntary associations do not necessarily owe their existence to the State, which is only *primus inter pares*. A Government which attacks a society because of its opinions has generally something to conceal. To give a State power to say what societies may be formed is to enable it to settle what criticism of the State will be allowed. Unity may be achieved, but it will be the unity of stagnation and decay.

The final argument against entrusting any authority, government, or any other body of persons, with a power to suppress opinions or men's freedom of action is suggested by Lord Acton in the remark: "Power corrupts and absolute power corrupts absolutely." The next two chapters will provide sufficient evidence of the truth of this statement. But it is important to bring out here that the principles which lie behind the doctrine of liberty of thought are just as urgent for democracy to keep in mind as for any other form of State. Supporters of a democratic form of government are apt to think that such a form is sufficient in itself as a guarantee of all desirable forms of individual liberty. But such is by no means the case.

Democracy under any definition requires that the will of the majority in a state shall in the long run dominate the policy of its government. Moreover, there is an almost universal tendency to estimate the truth of an opinion according to the number of those supporting it. This tendency is naturally strongest wherever the doctrine of the sovereignty of the people prevails. Yet a moment's thought will suffice to show that there is no logical connection between the validity of a statement and the number of those making it. There is no divine right of majorities to interfere with the freedom of individuals or minorities. If democracy is to be successful, and to progress, it must respect, and imbibe more deeply, these principles of liberty. Democracy and liberty must go hand in hand; neither is complete without the other. Yet to-day they are too apt to be mutually exclusive.

It must here be added that nothing in these principles of liberty has any connection with the right and the liberty to own property. The right of individuals to private property is desirable in small measure to allow them to express their personalities. Nevertheless, this right ceases when the livelihood of other individuals comes into question. The nature of property alters in quality where it has altered in quantity beyond a certain degree. Vast property, it is widely conceded, gives such power over human lives to a few individuals that the political liberty of the controlled becomes largely irrelevant. Thus the security of individual freedom may, in fact, largely depend upon the measure of economic equality that men are willing to organize. This will be briefly touched upon in a later part of this essay.

These principles form part of the case for freedom of conscience. In so far as acting according to the dictates of conscience involves expressing opinions conscientiously held or organizing to try to get these opinions realized in action, e.g. by some change in the law, the general principles of liberty are obviously applicable.

The question arises, however, as to when is one justified in disobeying a State and resisting its will. Is a member of a religious body which does not believe in medical aid to be allowed to let his wife die, when medical aid would have saved her, on the ground that to call in a doctor was contrary to his conscience? Is a parent to be permitted not to send his child to school, because it is contrary to his conscience? It is undeniable that at some point resistance to the State may become a duty. Again and again through history progress has been achieved, as will be shown in the following chapters, by individuals who defied the majority opinion and the State. But such a step is usually the result of injustice and would not be taken if there was any other way of calling attention to the need for change. An individual or a group of individuals will not as a rule take such a grave step as to resist the State unless there is some compelling cause, and under those circumstances it is the State or majority opinion which will be at fault and not the persons who defy it. The General Strike of 1926 did not take place until the trade unions felt there was no other way of calling the attention of the Government and the public to the suffering of the miners. The surest way under such circumstances to restore the stability of the State is to remedy the injustice. It should perhaps be added that treachery or treason to the State is occasioned by quite different motives and no word said here has any application to it.

The compulsion of conscience which a State exercises should be an educative compulsion and not a mere outward coercion degrading both those who use it and those on whom it is used. It has recently been said,[1] "If our moral consciousness asserts that some act is wrong, or some institution is bad, it makes this assertion in obedience to some fundamental human and spiritual value that is being set at nought. If, after the most serious consideration, we are clear as to this pronouncement, we have no option but to obey. It carries its own authority with it." With the highest moral decisions, decisions of conscience made after full thought and with full knowledge, it is

[1] Francis E. Pollard, *War and Human Values.*

denied that the State has a right to interfere. This claim of interference is denied most strenuously of all when questions of life and death are involved. The conscientious objector denies the right of the State to compel men to kill.

In the end the basic principle uniting the principles of liberty with the necessity for freedom of conscience will be found to be the value of the individual. "He is no abstraction. He exists in a sense that no State does. If deeds are to be done, he does them; if agony is to be endured, he endures it. The State was made for man, not man for the State. The seed of community found in man's common qualities and needs and in the necessities of partnership has flowered in many associations and institutions which seek to serve the good of their members. The State is but one of these, and from the especial nature of its position, its automatic continuance and its compulsory powers, it requires most of all that we test it constantly by the principle that its *raison d'être* is to contribute to individual well-being."[1]

[1] F. E. Pollard, op. cit.

Chapter 3

A SURVEY OF PERSECUTION

Some had name, and fame, and honour; learnèd they were,
and wise and strong;
Some were nameless, poor, unlettered, weak in all but
grief and wrong.
Named and nameless, all live in us: one and all they lead
us yet,
Every pain to count for nothing, every sorrow to forget.

WILLIAM MORRIS

The first well-known case of persecution for the sake of conscience is that of Socrates. Socrates was charged with not believing in the gods whom the community recognized and with introducing other new deities, and it was added that he had corrupted the youth. In his reply Socrates (as quoted by Professor Bury[1]) asserted that the individual conscience was supreme over all human law. He said: "If you propose to acquit me on condition that I abandon my search for truth, I will say, I thank you O Athenians, but I will obey God who has, I believe, set me this task rather than you, and so long as I have breath and strength I will never cease from my occupation with philosophy. I will continue the practice of accosting whomsoever I may and saying to him—'Are you not ashamed of setting your heart on wealth and honours while you have no care for wisdom and truth and making your soul better?' I know not what death is —it may be a good thing—and I am not afraid of it, but I do know that it is a bad thing to desert one's post and I prefer what may be good to what I know to be bad." Insisting on the

[1] *Short History of the Freedom of Thought* (Home University Library Thornton Butterwoth).

value of free discussion, he said: "I am a sort of gadfly, given to the State by God; and the State is a great and noble steed who is tardy in his motions owing to his very size and requires to be stirred into life. I am that gadfly which God has attached to the State."

Socrates then had a chance of escaping, but he preferred not to do this as he considered that without the State's consent it would be wrong. The majority of the Athenians believed that it was necessary that Socrates should die for interests of the State, and he is one of the first martyrs of whom we have a record who suffered for the sake of conscience and for the sake of freedom of expression of opinion. He makes no distinction between the two. His conscience tells him that he must express his views even if they appear subversive and seditious. He believes that the expression of his views is good for the State and necessary for the well-being of the people.

It may, however, be noted that if he had been tried in a later age he might have fared worse. As Sir John MacDonell says[1]:—

"Brought before an ecclesiastical Court, as were Bruno and Campanella, he would have been tortured; he would have been subjected to repeated examinations and long confinement intended to break him down in body; his prosecutors laying hold of his belief in a demonic voice, he would have been charged with sorcery or magic; he would have been cut off from his disciples and delivered over, shattered and crushed in body, to the civil power to be burned. Had he been tried in this country at any time before the middle of last century, would his treatment have been much better? In Tudor or Stuart reigns he would have been charged for high treason or blasphemy or misdemeanour of some kind, browbeaten by the law officers prosecuting, scolded by the presiding judge as a pestilent nuisance in the State, and his last words before a cruel death might have been cut short or drowned in the roll of drums beneath the

[1] Sir John MacDonell's *Historical Trials* (by permission of the Clarendon Press, Oxford)

32

scaffold. Let us picture him coming before an English or a Scotch judge at the end of the eighteenth or the beginning of the nineteenth century—before an Ellenborough who tried Hone, or a Braxfield who tried Muir, and Margarot; he would have been belaboured with pompous platitudes or subjected to coarse ribaldry, and his conviction would have been certain."

Sir John MacDonell was writing in 1911, but what of the last twenty years? It is illuminating to consider what would have been the reaction of a totalitarian regime to the Socratic method. In England the philosopher might have been charged with sedition or blasphemy, or, in recent years, with insulting words or behaviour under the Public Order Act, 1936.

The Greek City-States on the whole, the Roman republic and early Empire tolerated all religions and all opinions. The Emperor Tiberius remarked, "If the Gods are insulted let them see to it themselves." An exception to this toleration was made in the case of Christianity. The intolerance of the Christians was well known and it was obvious they claimed freedom exclusively for themselves. The Roman Empire seems to have been faced with somewhat the same problem as faces modern democracies, namely, whether in the name of freedom it should tolerate a movement which would abolish freedom. The Roman Emperors took the course of attempting to suppress Christianity, and although there is no doubt that Christian apologists have grossly exaggerated the sufferings of the early martyrs, an attempt was made to suppress them with cruelty and in a spirit which denied the principles of liberty. Even Marcus Aurelius, one of the most liberal and cultivated Emperors, and one whose writings on the conduct of life are still read and valued, allowed some persecution. The Christians were only interested in freedom of conscience for themselves. As Professor Bury puts it, "The martyrs died for conscience but not for liberty."

The Christians attained freedom of conscience by a toleration decree issued by the pagan Emperor Galerius in A.D. 311. A similar decree was issued by the Christian Emperor Constantine, but soon after they obtained power they abandoned their belief in freedom of conscience and set themselves to suppress every other religion.

There ensued a period described by Professor Bury as the period of "Reason in Prison" or what is commonly known as the Dark Ages. Yet heresy—so called—arose in one part of Christendom after another, and, although suppressed, arose again and again in varying forms.

The persecution of the Albigeois who lived in South-West France is well known. They refused to take oaths or to take human life on any ground, and when Pope Innocent III found a severe decline in his revenue from this district he announced a crusade against them, and those who took part were offered absolution from all their sins.

The Inquisition was established in 1233, and a machinery of persecution was after some time set up in every State. This arm of the Church did not itself burn the heretics, but handed them over to the secular power. Joan of Arc, one of the most notable of all its victims, refused to deny what her inner voice or conscience told her was right, and in the interests of the English power in France she was burnt as a heretic and a blasphemer. The Court of Inquisition which tried her appears to have been entirely under English influence at that date, and when that power was removed from France the decision was reversed.

The effect of the imprisonment of reason was effectively to obstruct the increase of human knowledge. The view was generally taken, for example, that disease was due to demons, and if this view was questioned the doubter was liable to be considered a heretic. Roger Bacon was imprisoned for a long while in the thirteenth century because he was too interested in scientific research.

But during the dark night of reason in Christian Europe, culture, science and freedom flourished in the Arab world, about which not nearly enough is known. It is, however, illuminatingly treated by Joseph McCabe in his *Splendour of*

Moorish Spain,[1] where he points out that, while Christian crusades were taking place against the heretics, under the Moors Christians and Jews were freely tolerated and flourished. Another feature of this Moslem rule was the freedom of women, who, in many cases, earned their own living, could own property and plead in Court. In England it was not until 1882 that a married woman could own her property free from any control of her husband. Ultimately, however, the Spanish Monarchy—at the instance of the Church—threw the Moors out of the country, and since this expulsion it is doubtful whether Spain has ever been so prosperous and cultured. The standard of education has been lower and intolerance has been much more marked. After the expulsion of the Moors the Inquisition had the field to itself. A prisoner before it was presumed to be guilty, and no Jews, Moors, servants or relations could give evidence for him. Every member of the population was required to be an informer, and a situation prevailed, similar to that now in Germany, where no one was free from the suspicion of even his own family.

Both the machinery of Church government and the feudal State united to repress the free workings of conscience. However, the Renaissance and the Reformation presented a growing challenge to both these organizations. It was inevitable that their reply should be by way of increased persecution.

The leaders of the Reformation did not believe in religious liberty and the right to freedom of conscience. They attempted indeed to set up other authorities in the place of the Roman Church. Nevertheless, their own revolt implied a principle which was bound in the end to lead to an increase of freedom. Some of the persecutions carried out by the Calvinists rival the brutalities of the Roman Catholic Church. Calvin attempted to govern Geneva not by democracy but by what is described as theocracy. Servetus, for instance, who had published theological views which for some reason annoyed Calvin, foolishly allowed himself to fall into Calvin's hands in Geneva and was charged

[1] Watts & Co.

with heresy. His trial was conducted with the usual lack of justice in these cases. So bitterly did his theological opponents hate him that one of the charges preferred against Servetus was that he had escaped from the prison of the Inquisition! In the end he was actually burnt for publishing theological books outside Geneva!

Other well-known martyrs of freedom and conscience are Bruno, who was burnt by the Roman Catholic Church for giving expression to heretical opinions, and Galileo, who was sentenced for maintaining that the earth moves round the sun. Valuable accounts of these trials can be read in Sir John McDonell's *Historical Trials*, where the procedure of the Inquisition is explained in some detail. No reader of this book can fail to note the similarity of trial under the Inquisition and that under dictatorships.

In England the first important heretical movement against the Church was that of the Lollards. In 1400 they were ferociously suppressed by the statute against heretics. Henry VIII impartially punished both Roman Catholics and Protestants, but the struggle for religious freedom—which in the sixteenth century represented the whole struggle for freedom—was carried on by the religious sects until the time of the Commonwealth. Then the Established Church was temporarily overthrown and a profusion of religious denominations flourished. Before continuing the story of resistance to oppression in this country, we must not forget the debt which humanity owes to the Netherlands for maintaining in dark days a tolerant regime, where some freedom of thought was possible and where scholars and thinkers found refuge and a chance to publish their books.

During the Commonwealth and the period of the Restoration much of the persecution for the sake of conscience was borne by the Society of Friends. Especially during the second period the Friends were prosecuted and flung into jail for refusing to serve in the Army, refusing to pay tithes, take oaths, and for holding their meetings of worship. In 1660 George Fox, the founder of the Society, was imprisoned for that "he was a person suspected to be a disturber of the Peace of the nation, a common enemy to His Majesty Our Lord the King, a chief upholder of the Quaker sect and that he, with others of his fanatical opinions have of late endeavoured to raise insurrections in this part of the country to the imbruing of the nation in blood." Fox in his reply stated that, "the postures of war I never learned" and that the term "fanatic" is more applicable to the "mad, furious, foolish spirit" that relies on force and persecution.[1]

Act after Act of Parliament was passed to suppress the Non-conformists and to prevent their holding their religious assemblies, but notwithstanding all distraints and imprisonments they continued to meet and maintain their testimony. A notable service to freedom was rendered by William Penn and William Meade in 1670, when they were charged with causing a riot and the jury returned a verdict, first of all, of "Not Guilty." After bullying from the Recorder and the Lord Mayor, they changed this to a verdict of "Guilty of speaking in Gracechurch Street." This was patently no verdict of "Guilty," and the jury were accordingly fined by the Recorder and imprisoned until the fines were paid; but on appeal it was established that no jury could be punished for its verdict. Thus was one more "freedom" established in English Constitutional Law.

The persecution of Dissent was not successful, although it drove many Friends and others to America, where it was hoped that greater freedom of conscience could be found.

This persecution ended with James II's proclamation of toleration suspending the brutal laws against persons who were not members of the Church of England. After Parliament had asserted its right to dethrone a king who behaved in an improper manner, William III came to the throne, and the Toleration Act was passed in 1689. The credit for this is due to William himself, to the Whigs, who had brought in a similar bill in 1680,

[1] *The Quakers in Peace and War* by M. E. Hirst (George Allen & Unwin, 3/6).

37

to the Church which could hardly ignore the promises it had made, but largely to the steadfastness of those who had suffered and the desire of the nation that strife should cease. Nor should the influence of John Locke's letter concerning Toleration be omitted. The preamble to this Act contains the words "for as much as some ease to scrupulous consciences, in the exercise of religion, may be an effectual means to unite Their Majesties Protestant subjects, in interest and affection." This is probably the first recognition by the legislature of the right of conscience. It is true that toleration was only given for religious opinions —and only to Protestants—but once the principle was recognized it was likely to be claimed for Roman Catholics and bound to be extended to the sphere of politics.

Later recognition by the legislature of the rights of conscience is to be found in some of the Oaths of Abjuration, which made the person taking the oath declare "in his conscience before God and the world."

The persecution of the Quakers for their religious opinions slackened after 1688, but never in time of war have they been free from it. Throughout the eighteenth century those who were seamen were liable to be seized by the Press gang. In 1694 Thomas Chalkley, as a boy of nineteen, was "seized near his Southwark home, brought on board ship and thrown into the hold, where his physical discomfort was overshadowed by his moral shrinking from the 'dark and hellish' conversation of his fellow prisoners. When the longed-for morning came and they were brought on deck, the lieutenant asked him whether he would serve the King.

" 'I answered that I was willing to serve him in my business, and according to my conscience; but as for war or fighting, Christ had forbid it in His excellent Sermon on the Mount; and for that reason I could not bear arms, nor be instrumental to destroy or kill men. Then the Lieutenant looked on me and on the people and said 'Gentlemen, what shall we do with this fellow? He swears he will not fight.' The Commander of the vessel made answer, 'No, no, he will neither swear nor fight.' Upon which they turned me on shore."

Throughout this period and especially during the long imperial wars in which the country was engaged and during the two Jacobite rebellions the Friends maintained their testimony against war and refused to serve in the Militia or to pay special war taxes such as that known as "trophy money." Special provisions were made by the Militia Acts for Quakers by laying it down that if they refused to serve their goods were to be distrained on to provide a substitute.

In 1776 Bernard Harrison was drawn for the Militia at Standen, Hertfordshire. He had no property on which distraints could be levied "save clothes." The magistrates on learning of his religious objection to the bearing of arms decided to send him to prison. The Friends took the matter up and obtained legal opinions which showed that this procedure was doubtful, and that the true principle would appear to be "that an Englishman cannot legally be deprived of his liberty without a positive direction in an Act of Parliament." Some five years later Lord Kenyon, in giving his opinion on the matter, said "It would be harsh measure if the legislature made any law pressing upon tender consciences, and if any clause affords two constructions it would be reasonable to adopt that construction which avoided so great severity." These legal opinions are sometimes forgotten. The principles they express can still be recalled with profit by Members of Parliament who lightly pass into law Defence of the Realm Acts, Emergency Powers Acts and Regulations restricting liberty, which make it plain that they have much less regard for it than some eighteenth-century statesmen.

During the same period increase in freedom was taking place in other parts of the British Empire. The Quaker State, Pennsylvania, was founded in 1681. It granted more liberty of conscience and worship than was enjoyed at that time either in Europe or America. Freedom was granted to all "who confess and acknowledge the one Almighty and Eternal God to be the

39

creator, upholder and ruler of the world, and hold themselves obliged in conscience to live justly and peaceably in civil society." Office holders were required to believe in Jesus Christ. In 1692 the Crown imposed a test which excluded Roman Catholics from office, but liberty of worship was maintained for all. The original constitution of the colony only provided the death penalty for the offences of treason and murder. Not enough attention has been paid to the practical ethical significance of the history of this State where, for some seventy years, liberty and freedom of conscience but no army were maintained. While other American Colonies were frequently engaged in wars with Indians, the Quaker colony of Pennsylvania had remained at peace with them because it treated the Indians as human beings. It will probably be convenient at this point to carry this account of persecution in America up to the Civil War.

After 1756 the Quaker control of the Colony ceased and the usual Militia Acts began to be passed. From that time onwards Quakers in Pennsylvania were persecuted, as in the rest of the Thirteen Colonies were those who refused to take part in war. Persecution occurred particularly during the American War of Independence.

In 1774 an address by Congress to the English nation said "we hold it essential to English liberty that no man be condemned unheard, or punished for a supposed offence without having an opportunity of making his defence." This principle was from time to time set at naught by the American authorities in their dealings with the Quakers, and it is well to recall it now as the modern State in England seems increasingly to disregard it.

It was during the War of 1811 that the clerk of Virginia Yearly Meeting memorialized the legislature of Virginia about the then existing Militia Law as follows:—

"In this enlightened age and country, and before this Legislature, your Memorialists conceive it unnecessary to urge the unalienable rights of conscience, or to adduce any arguments to show that the relations between man and his Creator, neither

40

can nor ought to be prescribed or controlled by any human authority. It is unnecessary, because the proposition is self evident, and especially because it is one of the fundamental principles, upon which the civil and political institutions of this country are established . . . the State itself, by its convention which ratified the federal constitution, expressly declared, that 'the liberty of conscience cannot be cancelled, abridged, restrained, or modified by any authority of the United States. . . . They therefore respectfully petition, that the laws imposing military requisitions and penalties for non-compliance, may be considered as they respect your petitioners, and such relief afforded as to the wisdom of the legislature shall seem just and necessary."

Persecution of conscientious objectors again occurred during the Civil War and the war of 1914–18. Mr. E. N. Wright in his admirable study of conscientious objection in the Civil War[1] shows how they received recognition from the authorities both of the South and of the North. Effort was made particularly by Secretary Stanton to provide for conscientious objectors and an Act of Congress of February 24, 1864, provided that conscientious objectors were to be considered as non-combatants and assigned for duty in hospitals or to the care of freedmen or to pay the sum of 300 dollars for the benefit of sick and wounded soldiers. This liberal minded law did not satisfy those who felt that military service or any substitute for it was wrong, and the following editorial from *The Friend* expresses this view which is of interest to-day in consideration of the difference between the absolutist and alternativist positions:—

"While, therefore, we fully appreciate the good motives which, we doubt not, prompted the adoption of the section above quoted, and hail it as a cheering indication of the advance of correct views upon this important subject, we do not see how it can relieve our members, or they consistently avail themselves of any of its provisions; inasmuch as to be sent into the hospitals or serve as nurses, etc., or to be assigned to the care of freedmen, is just as

[1] Pennsylvania Press, 1931.

much a penalty imposed for obeying the requisitions of our religion in not performing military service, as is the fine of three hundred dollars. It matters not whether the commutation for military service is money or personal service in some other department; in either case it is an assumption on the part of the government of a right to oblige the subject to violate his conscience, or to exact a penalty if he elects to obey God rather than man."

We must now return to the history of liberty in England in the eighteenth century. The subject of police search will first engage our attention.

At home about 1763 Wilkes began a notable struggle for liberty in his paper *The North Britain*, in one issue of which it was insinuated that George III had made himself party to a deliberate falsehood. In order to collect evidence of this the Secretary of State issued warrants for the search of Wilkes's house. Warrants which authorized a general search of premises for evidence of any crime had from time to time been issued before this, but in 1765 in a case arising out of the proceedings against Wilkes the Law Courts declared them to be illegal. This decision remained one of the corner stones of English liberty until 1934. In order to give a proper picture to the reader the history and the present position of police powers of search will be treated here and not in Chapters VI and VII. In 1934 it was decided by the High Court that, although the Police have no power to search the premises of an arrested person without a warrant (but articles in his possession relevant to the charge can be taken), yet if they come across evidence of some other offence (whether committed by the accused or anyone else) they will be excused from an illegal act if they seize this other evidence. The Royal Commission on Police Powers and Procedure in 1929 stated that "it had long been the practice of the police to search a dwelling of a person for whose arrest a warrant has been issued, and in cases of arrest without warrant, to search premises as well as the arrested person in cases of serious crime where it appears that material evidence is likely to be obtained." There was no specific Act of Parliament authorizing this, although the view was expressed by the representatives of the Home Office that it had by long use become part of the common law. The Home Office view was wrong. The mere passage of time will not purge a particular practice of its illegality.

The Royal Commission stated that it was a matter of some concern to them that the police should have to rely on powers of which the legality was doubtful or obscure, and recommended that the situation should be cleared up. Needless to say, nothing has been done about this recommendation of the Royal Commission, or about most of their other recommendations. It is to be hoped that some Member of Parliament will some day have the energy and courage to press for the carrying into effect of the whole of the Royal Commission's Report.

The Defence Regulations made under the Emergency Powers (Defence) Act, 1939, now provide that if a Justice of the Peace is satisfied that there is a reasonable ground for suspecting the commission of an offence against any of the Regulations or the performance of *any act* prejudicial to the public safety or the defence of the realm, and that evidence of this is to be found at any specified premises, he may grant a search warrant authorizing *any persons*, including members of the armed forces, to enter and search the premises and every person found there or who is believed to have recently left or is about to enter the premises. Moreover there is power to seize any article which is reasonably believed to be evidence of such act or crime. Powers of search have from time to time been conferred upon the police by numerous Acts of Parliament particularly in cases such as those where persons are suspected of receiving stolen goods, but have rarely been granted in cases of political offences. It is obvious, however, that such warrants can now be granted to seize political books and literature. Moreover if a Superintendent of Police, or any authorized person, considers that it is *expedient* in the interests

43

of the State on the ground of urgency or other good cause that premises should be searched forthwith, he can order the premises to be searched without a search warrant from a magistrate. There is also power to detain any person against whom evidence is found by a search. Search must still be exercised in respect of particular premises and by named persons but search warrants are much more general than they were before 1939.

Having outlined the history of the police powers of search up to the present day, it is necessary to turn again to the end of the eighteenth century to review in the same way the history of freedom of opinion. Throughout the period following the French Revolution of 1789 down to the passing of the Reform Bill in 1832 there was savage persecution by the Government of expressions of opinion. It is not possible in the compass of this book to give much of the detail of the struggle. Those who would read further on this subject may be referred to W. H. Wickwar's *The Struggle for Freedom of the Press*[1] and to *Penalties upon Opinion*[2] by H. P. Bonner. The English Government in this period used all the old weapons of the criminal law, and if these were not sufficient they passed new Acts of Parliament. Particular effort was made to suppress Thomas Paine's *Age of Reason*, and Richard Carlile was prosecuted again and again for publishing this book and similar papers. When he went to prison his wife took his place. She was sentenced to imprisonment, and his sister, who took her place, soon followed her. Various employees succeeded them and when they went to prison, volunteers from all over the country came up to continue publication. At one time there were eight of Carlile's shopmen in prison in addition to the three Carliles themselves.

The offence of all these was the old one of "blasphemous libel," which dates from the early seventeenth century. Before that time offenders were usually charged with heresy. Those interested can read a full account in Mrs. Bonner's *Penalties upon Opinion*.

[1] George Allen & Unwin, 7s. 6d.
[2] Thinker's Library, Watts & Co., 1s. 3d.

It is important to recall the Blasphemy Act, 1698, for this is still in force. According to this statute it is illegal for any person who has been educated as a Christian, or who has at any time professed the Christian religion, by any printing, writing, teaching or speaking, to:—(a) assert there are more gods than one or (b) deny the Christian religion to be true or (c) deny the Scriptures of the Old and New Testaments to be of divine authority. The penalty for a first offence against this Act is to be held incapable of holding any office or employment whether ecclesiastical, civil or military. For a second offence the penalty is imprisonment for three years. It is doubtful if this Act has ever been enforced, but Parliament has refused to repeal it, and it could at any time be used to suppress a person who thought he should use the liberty of expressing his opinion to criticize Christianity. This is surely offensive to modern Christian opinion.

The nature of blasphemy and blasphemous libel, which are Common Law offences, has varied from time to time. Prosecutions for this offence were probably most frequent between 1789 and 1830 and at this date blasphemy was the crime of attacking Christianity. It was never a crime to attack any other religion. It was during this period that Shelley was prevented by the Law Courts from having possession of his children on the ground that he was an atheist and had published blasphemous works. It was illegal to leave money by will to agnostic societies until 1917. Charles Bradlaugh, the famous nineteenth-century free-thinker, was prosecuted in 1882 for blasphemous libel, but he was acquitted. From this date the law of blasphemy changed, Lord Coleridge denying that Christianity was any longer part of the Law of England. Prosecutions for blasphemy are now rare. If the offence is committed, it is generally dealt with under some other Act of Parliament. It now consists in using such scurrilous language regarding Christianity as might exasperate the feelings of others and so occasion a breach of the peace—not necessarily at the time the words are used. As recently as 1930, Parliament refused to pass a Bill abolishing the blasphemy laws, although they are manifestly inconsistent with the principles of liberty and freedom of opinion. Christianity, like every other institution, must learn to meet criticism by reasoned argument. If a breach of the peace actually takes place, it can be dealt with under the ordinary criminal law. The law as it is remains as an expression of religious intolerance.

One of the most discreditable episodes in the history of the House of Commons occurred in 1882, when Charles Bradlaugh, an atheist and Republican and the elected Member for Northampton, claimed the right to affirm instead of taking the oath. The House of Commons first refused to allow him to affirm and then to take the oath, and when he persisted in trying to do so it sent him to the Clock Tower. He was three times re-elected and thrice excluded by Parliament. Prejudice and bigotry swayed the House of Commons until 1885 when the new Speaker permitted him to take his seat. In 1888 the House passed Bradlaugh's Affirmation Bill. When he was dying in 1891 the House of Commons carried a resolution expunging from its journals the derelict resolutions of the past excluding him, but the dying man was then unconscious and he did not live to know of this general acknowledgment of his right.

After being for long the main issue at stake, the struggle for religious freedom became towards the end of the seventeenth century only one aspect of the subject. Like the subjects of the right of search, blasphemy and freedom of opinion, it deserves a separate account.

So complete is the religious freedom which we now enjoy that English men are apt to forget the harsh laws which were in force until just over one hundred years ago. Those which survived the Toleration Act 1689, excluded Nonconformists from all Universities, from all municipal corporations and all public and civil service offices, and some were excluded from juries. It is true that the practice grew up in the eighteenth century of passing Acts of Indemnity to indemnify persons who had taken office without swearing the oaths prescribed by these Acts, but this was not considered satisfactory. Repeal of the laws against Nonconformity took place gradually throughout the nineteenth century but was virtually complete by the middle. Compulsory payment of tithes to the Established Church was converted in 1836 into a compulsory money payment. Quakers from the foundation of their Society to 1836 had constantly refused to pay tithes, because it was against their conscience, and had, as their records show, continually had their goods seized and sold and sometimes been completely ruined. These particularly benefited by the change. The money payment was made a charge on land and there was no reason why it should not be paid. Compulsory rates for the Church of England were not abolished until 1868—and only then in the face of great opposition. Religious freedom for the Nonconformists may be said to have been substantially attained as from 1871 when the Universities were freed, although as long as the Established Church exists with its endowments, part of which represent public property, religious equality cannot be said to be complete.

The laws against the Roman Catholics were much severer. It was high treason in England for any priest or Jesuit to remain in the country three days without taking the Oath of Supremacy: it was high treason for any Catholic to convert a Protestant and for any Protestant to be converted. An Act of 1700 offered £100 for the discovery of any Priest found in the Kingdom; such a priest was then to be perpetually imprisoned. To hear Mass was punishable with one year's imprisonment. Catholics were prohibited from taking lands by purchase, inheritance, or in any other way, prohibited from owning a horse worth more than £5, from keeping arms and from living in London when they had any other place of residence. In Ireland the laws were severer still. Under an Act of 1704 the son of a Roman Catholic who became a Protestant could claim all his father's land to the exclusion of all the other children. Catholic education was strictly prohibited. The complete failure of these laws shows that a State cannot in the long run suppress opinions which are conscientiously held.

As the eighteenth century progressed the laws were less and less enforced and the first relief came with two Acts of 1788 and 1791. The most important Act for the relief of Roman Catholics, was that of 1829 which was passed partly because Wellington and Peel were afraid of the threatened violence in Ireland and partly because the Commons were genuinely convinced of the need for it. However, one hundred and ninety thousand Irish forty-shilling freeholders, most of whom had voted for O'Connell, the first professed Catholic M.P. since the seventeenth century, were by the same Act disfranchised. Nor did the Act give complete freedom to Catholics: it imposed restrictions on Jesuits and members of monastic orders, restrictions which were offensive although they remained a dead letter. It was not until 1919 that the Law Courts declared it legal to leave money for the purposes of having masses said for a deceased's soul. Only two years before, the House of Lords had for the first time declared it legal to leave property to a rationalist or agnostic society. Not until 1926 were the restrictions on Roman Catholics imposed by the Act of 1829 finally repealed.

The cause of liberty is always progressing or regressing—it never stands still. Up to 1914 there are frequent set-backs but steady progress. From 1870 to 1914 English liberty was probably at its maximum. The liberty of Nonconformists and Roman Catholics had substantially been secured. This period saw an alteration in the law of blasphemy, the right won for free-thinkers to sit in Parliament, and to affirm if they objected to taking the oaths of office. For the trade unions liberty was won by acts of 1871, 1875 and finally in 1906.

Legal decisions established the right of public meetings in the street, and it seemed to all men that progress must go on and that liberty would broaden down from precedent to precedent. Yet even in this period liberty was attacked both at home and in Ireland. Irish Coercion Acts taking away fundamental liberties were frequently passed. The spirit of bigotry and intolerance which still subsisted was shown by the persecution of Bradlaugh.

A Liberal writer in 1887 said ". . . The cloven-hoof of tyranny is seen everywhere. We find it in the partisanship of the Speaker of the House of Commons; in the high Tory harangues of the Tory judges; in the brutality of *The Times* newspaper; in the rascally harrying of Glasgow Liberal Clubs unchecked by the guardians of public order; in the violent dispersal of loyal processions; in the hampering of free public meetings; in these we find it in England. But in Ireland it is simply rampant. There law no longer exists—the will of the Executive has taken its place. Balfour is King, Lords and Commons at one and the same time. His nod is law. The time he can spare from golf he devotes to purging the poison of liberty from the hearts of the Irish people by the prison cell or the policeman's bullet. And this foul and virulent disease bids fair to destroy the freedom even of England unless a radical cure be administered."[1] The reader should note the vigorous language and ask himself what would be the results to-day for an author who employed a similar style in political polemics.

One of the fundamental principles of the British Constitution that there should be no taxation without representation was denied to half the community. A woman might not vote nor hold public office. Governments prevaricated and drove them in the end to the violence of the Suffragette movement. The demand was for justice and they answered it by forcible feeding in prison.

The people of England, taken on the whole, had more liberty during this time to express their opinions and to advocate changes in society than they had ever had before, but the incidents narrated and other events showed that this liberty was by no means secure. The words of Professor L. T. Hobhouse, writing

[1] *The Proper Limits of Obedience to the Law*, by Robert Spence Watson, LL.D.

in 1904, "that in public affairs there is a current which sweeps us backward when we think to rest upon our oars," had been forgotten. Liberty was taken for granted but with the war of 1914 there came a rude awakening and to this we now turn.

Chapter 4

LIBERTY IN CHAINS, 1914–1918

As long as you have the wisdom to keep the sovereign authority of this country as the sanctuary of liberty, the sacred temple consecrated to our common faith, wherever the chosen race and sons of England worship freedom, they will turn their faces towards you. The more they multiply, the more friends you will have; the more ardently they love liberty the more perfect will be their obedience. Slavery they can have anywhere. It is a weed that grows in every soil. They may have it from Spain, they may have it from Prussia. But until you become lost to all feeling of your true interest and your natural dignity, freedom they can have from none but you. This is the commodity of price of which you have the monopoly. . . . It is the spirit of the English Constitution, which, infused through the mighty mass, pervades, feeds, unites, invigorates, vivifies every part of the Empire, even down to the minutest member.

BURKE

The first twentieth-century war to end wars, which began in August, 1914, gave the enemies of liberty their best chance for a hundred years, and they took full advantage of it. The attack on liberty of conscience came from the Military Service Acts and on freedom of opinion from the Defence of the Realm Acts. The men responsible adopted Strafford's motto "Thorough" —and they who passed the Military Service Acts and D.O.R.A. gave their successors.

The author acknowledges a great debt to a small booklet

entitled *British Freedom, 1914 to 1917*, which was issued by th
National Council for Civil Liberties in 1917.[1]

We will consider first the attacks upon the freedom of the Press
Milton said in his *Areopagitica*, "truth is compared in Scriptur
to a streaming fountain: if her waters flow not in perpetua
progression they sink into a muddy pool of conformity an
tradition." Milton's powerful plea for freedom for printing, an
the arguments he uses, are as strong to-day as they were in 1644
when he wrote. He points out that no man is infallible and ye
that a censorship assumes that certain men have the last wor
as to what is true. He reminds would-be censors that if they d
suppress some evil, at the same time they are bound to suppres
some good. He reminds his reader that the effect of any censor
ship of literature and printing is to promote mediocre writin,
and to discourage original thought. But those who imposed th
censorship of this time were not troubled by such possibilities
Regulation 27 under D.O.R.A. made it an offence for any perso
"by word of mouth, or in writing or in any . . . printed publi
cation" to:

(*a*) Spread false reports or make false statements; or
(*b*) Spread reports or make statements calculated or likely t
 cause disaffection to His Majesty or to interfere wit
 the success of H.M.'s Allies by land or sea, or to preju
 dice H.M.'s relations with foreign powers; or
(*c*) Spread reports or make statements intended or likely t
 prejudice the training, discipline, or administration o
 any of H.M.'s Forces.

Matter submitted to the Press Bureau of the Governmen
and which had been approved by them was protected fron
prosecution under this regulation. It is naturally not suggeste
that the activities mentioned were permissible. For our purpose
the vagueness of the language employed is the significant thing

[1] NOTE.—This Council ceased to exist after the 1914–18 war, but
similar body with the same title was formed in 1934.

pening the way, as it actually did, to the suppression of opinions and political thought which were disliked by the authorities. One of the effects of this regulation was the suppression of news of strikes. In December, 1916, two strikes were in progress: the one in Liverpool was settled on Government terms. The larger one was not, and was not even mentioned in the local paper. The censor systematically suppressed statements which gave the employees' point of view and only semi-official statements giving the employers' point of view were given to the Press.

It is stated that "in 1916 *Forward*, the Glasgow Socialist paper, was suppressed for no obvious reason except that of publishing a substantially true account of Mr. Lloyd George's Christmas visit to Glasgow, an account that differed from the official statement of the Ministry of Munitions. A few such incidents were quite enough to make most editors exclude from their columns any but the most violently bellicose views."

The *Bystander* was prosecuted for a cartoon with the title "Home Service," showing a man wheeling a perambulator. This prosecution was for printing matter "likely to prejudice recruiting and discipline."

As regards news of foreign affairs, the author of *British Freedom* stated in 1917: "The whole development of political conditions in Russia has been steadily concealed. The Tsar and his Ministers were extolled and their sins of omission and commission passed by in decorous silence, until—presto!—the British public woke one morning and rubbed its eyes to find there had been a revolution. 'The king is dead; long live the King!' It was then further discovered that this set of reactionaries were pro-Germans who had been stifling the loyal and eager forces of Russia and came within an ace of losing the war. It was a poor satisfaction to reflect that the Liberals of Russia had been strong enough to overthrow this corrupt tyranny in spite of the moral support so freely offered it by the trained Press of Britain, and the kindly cloak thrown over its nakedness by our censorship. Even the conditions in Ireland, both before the rebellion and

53

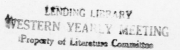

at the present time, have been hidden from public knowledge. In all these topics, it will be observed, knowledge is essential to the formation of any opinion of value on fundamental questions of public policy. In almost all cases the facts are published in neutral papers, and are evidently known to the enemy."

The Government promised that the censorship would not be applied to repress expressions of opinion, but in December, 1915, the Suffragette paper, *Britannia*, was suppressed because it published an attack on Sir Edward Grey's foreign policy.

Regulation 27 was then amended so as to make it an offence for any person to have in his possession, or on his premises, any document, the publication of which would be contrary to the previous clauses of the Regulation, unless he could prove either that he was ignorant, or that he had no intention of circulating the document to other persons. J. B. Bailey was given three months' imprisonment for writing (not publishing or even showing to another person) something against militarism. The judge declared that if it had been shown that he intended to do harm the maximum penalty would have been the death sentence.

However, the authorities were still not satisfied. A Regulation therefore followed forbidding the publication, without leave of the censor, of pamphlets dealing with the war or the making of peace. This regulation was carefully considered by the "Meeting for Sufferings," the executive body of the Society of Friends, who drew up, in December 1917, the following vindication of free speech:

"The Executive Body of the Society of Friends, after serious consideration, desires to place on record its conviction that the portion of the recent regulations requiring the submission to the Censor of all leaflets dealing with the present war and the making of peace, is a grave danger to the national welfare. The duty of every good citizen to express his thoughts on the affairs of his country is hereby endangered, and further, we believe that Christianity requires the toleration of opinions not our own, lest we should unwittingly hinder the workings of the spirit of God.

"Beyond this there is a deeper issue involved. It is for Christians a paramount duty to be free to obey, and to act and speak in accord with the law of God, a law higher than that of any State, and no Government official can release men from this duty.

"We realize the rarity of the occasions on which a body of citizens find their sense of duty to be in conflict with the law, and it is with a sense of the gravity of this decision that the Society of Friends must on this occasion act contrary to the regulation, and continue to issue literature on war and peace without submitting it to the Censor. It is convinced that in thus standing firm for spiritual liberty it is acting in the best interest of the nation."

The intention of the Society of Friends to continue to publish leaflets without the leave of the Censor was publicly announced, and in due course the Chairman and Secretaries of the Friends Service Committee were prosecuted for publishing the leaflet entitled *A Challenge to Militarism*, which consisted of information about conscientious objectors in prison. The prosecution took place in the Guildhall, and it is well known how, while the verdict was being considered, Friends in Court held a meeting for worship. The sentence on the two men defendants was six months' imprisonment each and on the woman defendant, Edith Ellis, £100 fine, 50 guineas costs, or three months imprisonment.

It will, of course, be said that in time of war freedom of expression of opinion must be curtailed. It is obvious that the publication of information likely to be useful to an enemy must be suppressed and the activities of persons who intentionally try to help the enemy must be frustrated. But it was not necessary on this ground to suppress the expression of pacifist or other genuine minority opinion. This opinion was ostensibly suppressed on the ground that it hindered the effective prosecution of the war, but in reality because the controllers of the war machine disliked any opposition.

It is necessary to remember that "power corrupts and absolute power corrupts absolutely." The case for the democratic conduct of a war has been expressed by no one better than by Professor Laski: "For once the right to criticize is withdrawn, the executive commits all the natural follies of dictatorship. It assumes a semi-divine character for its acts. It deprives the people of information essential to a proper judgment of its policy. It misrepresents the situation it confronts by that art of propaganda which, Mr. Cornford has happily said, enables it to deceive its friends without deceiving its enemies. A people in war time is always blind to the facts of its position and anxious to believe only agreeable news; the government takes care to provide it only with the news that is pleasant. If no such news is at hand it will be manufactured. Petty successes will be magnified into resounding victories; defeats will be minimized, wherever possible. The agony of the troops will be obscured by the clouds of censorship. A war-time government is always obtuse to suggestion, angry when inquiry is suggested, careless of truth. It can, in fact, only be moralized to the degree to which it is subject to critical examination in every aspect of its policy. And to penalize, therefore, the critic is not only to poison the moral foundations of the State, but to make it extremely difficult, when peace comes, for both government and the mass of citizens to resume the habits of normal decency."[1]

Events succeeding the war of 1914–18 most vividly confirmed these assertions. Public lack of knowledge of the secret treaties helped to produce the so-called Peace of Versailles. Lie after lie had been told about Germany and in a poisoned atmosphere the Peace Treaty was made. We now are reaping the fruits of a Treaty which was the result of a dictatorship in England between 1914 and 1918.

That dictatorship prevented the House of Commons from seeing German periodicals, although English newspapers were freely obtainable in Germany. That dictatorship thought i

[1] *Liberty in the Modern State*, by Professor H. J. Laski.

legitimate to encourage organized hooliganism to break up meetings of bodies whose opinions it did not approve. *British Freedom* stated in 1917: "The interference with the right of public and private meetings is due without exception to the abuse of positions of authority and power—to the activities (or inactivities) of editors, professors, the police, town councillors, Lords-Lieutenant and so on. In no case, so far as we are aware, has there been any interference with any meeting which was not assiduously and laboriously fomented from 'above' by the efforts of such persons." Attacks on meetings, which were not even pacifist, apparently received the support of the authorities. "The most scandalous example," continued this record, "of these attacks upon free speech was the break-up of the meeting of the U.D.C. at the Memorial Hall, Farringdon Street, in November, 1915. This outburst of hooliganism was incited by the Anti-German Union and certain organs of the London Press, in particular a well-known daily, whose editor has been distinguished for this sort of patriotism. The most sinister feature of this episode was the introduction of soldiers into the hall by means of forged tickets, together with the defence of the action of the military by the Under-Secretary for War. The War Office, for some reason quite unexplained, had sent down a representative to attend this meeting, whose report was one tissue of misrepresentations. In his speech incorporating this report, Mr. Tennant concluded with words that breathed the very spirit of Zabern: 'I had to back up the military, whom I hope I shall never desert in any matter of this kind when any allegation is brought against them.' Whether the allegation is true or false is evidently a matter to which the War Office is indifferent."

In 1916 a new regulation was made giving power to prohibit any meeting in a public place if it was likely to cause grave disorder, such as to make undue demands upon the police or military forces, and this power might be exercised by any authorized Mayor, Magistrate, or Chief Officer of Police—a precedent which, in September, 1939, was found useful by the authors of the defence regulations of that date. Meetings in Manchester and elsewhere to discuss high food prices were prohibited. In Cardiff a meeting of the National Council for Civil Liberties was broken up by an organized crowd which gained admission to the hall because the police refused to allow the doors to be shut. The Council for Civil Liberties called another meeting, but when arrangements were made to break this up, the Welsh miners threatened to strike if the meeting was prevented either by violence or Government action, and the railwaymen declared that they would refuse to bring any special train to Merthyr, as the wreckers of the Cardiff meeting were so conveyed from Birmingham.

It is sometimes said that while public expression of opinion was curtailed, it was possible to say in private what one liked. But a bus conductor who in conversation with a passenger used the words "We are fighting for royalty," together with similar sentiments, received two months' imprisonment. So did a Socialist member of the Stafford Board of Guardians for venturing anti-war sentiments in conversation at a military hospital. A man who said in Hyde Park that a horse is treated better than an ordinary private was given six months for "making statements likely to prejudice recruiting."

To the 1914–18 dictatorship it was an offence to possess papers which might be prejudicial to recruiting, and any pacifist or member of the No-Conscription Fellowship was liable to have his house searched to see if he had illegal literature.

"It has mattered little to the magistrate in many cases that there was no obvious intention if distributing the offending documents, or that the defendant produced evidence or made declarations to the effect that he did not intend to distribute them, although the intention to distribute and not the mere possession is what constituted the offence. Thus E. Driffil, of Bradford, was fined £10 for possession of certain leaflets which he declared on oath that he did not intend to distribute. In the prosecution of Councillor Kneeshaw of Birmingham, the evidence was as follows:

MAGISTRATE: "Did you see any machinery for distributing these documents?"

WITNESS (Police Constable): "Yes, sir, unaddressed envelopes."

Yet Mr. Philip Snowden, M.P., was not prosecuted when he challenged the Home Secretary to prosecute him for possessing the same leaflets for which others had been prosecuted.

One of the safeguards of English liberty has been that offences against the ordinary law of the land have been tried by civil courts. Serious cases are tried by judge and jury and minor offences before magistrates. Soldiers and sailors subject to military law and discipline have been tried by courts martial, but civilians could not be tried by courts martial since the Petition of Right, 1628.

One of the astonishing features of the D.O.R.A. regulations was a right given to the prosecution in the case of Press and munitions offences to decide that the case might be tried before a court martial. It must be borne in mind that the military situation gave no justification at all for such a course. In most other cases it was for the military authority to decide whether a case could be properly tried by a magistrate. The objectionable features of these arrangements were:

(1) the right given to the prosecution to decide before which Court a person should be tried and (2) the provision that civilians might be tried by courts martial for offences against the ordinary criminal law. Right to trial by jury was by these means considerably curtailed. The case of Roger Casement shows that it is not safe to give the prosecution powers which should be impartially exercised. Roger Casement, who was condemned to death for treason, had his appeal dismissed by the Court of Criminal Appeal. He was prosecuted by the Attorney-General, the late Lord Birkenhead, and the Attorney-General's consent had to be obtained before an appeal could be made to the House of Lords.

Although a very important point of law was involved Lord Birkenhead refused to consent to the appeal. It should be noted also that courts martial were given power to deal with offences against the regulations which concerned freedom and expression of opinion. These restrictions were too much for some Members of Parliament, and a bill amending the Defence of the Realm Act was introduced, and passed in March 1915 on the initiative of Lord Parmoor which restored the right of trial by jury except in cases of civil tumult.

There is no space here to deal with the trials which took place in secret, although it was an obvious abuse of the regulation when the prosecution of the I.L.P. paper the *Labour Leader*, was held in camera.

In peace time, by common law and the Habeas Corpus Acts, the law provides that any person who is illegally imprisoned can be freed. If any Englishman or foreigner is wrongfully imprisoned in this country the High Court will issue a writ of Habeas Corpus and the imprisoned person will then be brought before the Court. The Court then inquires whether he has committed any criminal offence or not, and if not will order him to be set free. For instance, in 1923 the Home Secretary, who had illegally deported two Irishmen to the Irish Free State, was ordered by the Court under this power to bring them back to England, as it was found they had been illegally detained and he was ordered to release them. Macaulay describes this writ as "the most stringent curb that ever legislature imposed on tyranny." One of the most important effects of this law is in preventing unlawful imprisonment from taking place. In wars and crises in English history previous to 1914, Habeas Corpus Acts had frequently been suspended by Parliament, but always by a Special Act and presumably Parliament had been fully aware of what it was doing.

However, during the years 1914–1918, the Government made a mere regulation empowering themselves to intern any person "of hostile origin, or association"—a vague phrase which could be interpreted at the Government's will, since no Law Court could inquire as to whether the Secretary of State, who ordered the internment, really thought it was necessary. The persons interned did not need to be guilty of any criminal offence and were not tried for any criminal offence. Under this regulation, moreover, British subjects were interned. *British Freedom* states that a man was interned because he was a "mere socialist agitator." The regulation was challenged in the Law Courts, the argument being that the Habeas Corpus Acts could not be suspended by a general power to make regulations for the defence of the realm, but only one Judge endorsed this view. Lord Shaw of Dunfermline said that "as the Act was construed, against regulations in their generality nothing can stand, no rights, be they as ancient as Magna Charta, no laws, be they as deep as the foundations of the Constitution. All are swept aside by the generality of the power vested in the Executive to issue 'regulations.' *Silent enim leges inter arma.*"

The new way of dealing with offenders was to be in Lord Shaw's words "No trial: proscription. The victim may be 'regulated'—not in his course of conduct or of action, not as to what he should do or avoid doing. He may be regulated to prison or the scaffold. . . . Vested with this power of proscription, and permitted to enter the sphere of opinion and belief they, who alone can judge as to public safety and defence, may reckon a political creed their special care and if that creed be socialism, pacifism, republicanism, the persons holding such creeds may be regulated out of the way, although never deed was done or word uttered by them that could be charged as a crime. The inmost citadel of our liberties would be thus attacked. For, as Sir Erskine May observes, this is 'the greatest of all our liberties—liberty of opinion.' "

During the war of 1914–18 there was one civil right which was more bitterly attacked than any of those whose fate has so far been considered. This was the right to have a conscience and to act upon it. In August, 1915, a National Register was taken, Parliament being told, when this Register was established, that it had nothing to do with conscription. Parliament appears to have swallowed this remarkable statement as it accepts other equally deceptive statements by Governments as to the intention of bills. It may, therefore, have been a surprise to some when in January, 1916, the first Military Service Act was introduced. All unmarried men from eighteen to forty-one were conscripted, but tribunals were set up to examine appeals for exemption on grounds of hardship and conscientious objection to the undertaking of combatant service. It was specifically laid down that a certificate of exemption could be absolute, for non-combatant service only, or on condition of engaging in work of national importance. Tribunals were appointed by local authorities and consisted of from five to twenty-five members. The large size of these tribunals was undoubtedly one of the reasons why they worked so badly. This was the first time that conscription of all the manhood of the nation was enforced in England. The conscience clause did show that the Government paid some attention to the value of freedom of conscience. It was significant, however, that the Government refused to accept a clause providing that the conscientious objector who got into the army should not have the death penalty inflicted on him. Some thirty-nine M.P.s voted against the bill, a much larger number than in 1939. From military to industrial conscription the stage was easy. Men who were pronounced medically unfit for the army were sent to a munitions factory in exchange for fit men, and had to sign forms stating that they understood they were liable to military service if they ever ceased to be employed on munitions. Mr. J. H. Thomas, on the 16th May, 1916, told the House of Commons of an employer who, when his men struck, reported them to the military, who at once recalled them to the colours.

J. W. Graham, in his valuable book *Conscription and Conscience*,[1] states that tribunals generally consisted of elderly local magnates or tradesmen—often with a Labour man who was known to be in favour of the war. They were regarded quite improperly as

[1] George Allen & Unwin, 1922. Unfortunately out of print.

being part of the administrative machinery of the Government. One of the worst features was the military representative who was there to object to every application and brow-beat and intimidate applicants. Not infrequently the military representative would retire with the tribunal when they were considering their decision. The Government, at the beginning did try to see that tribunals dealt with their cases fairly, instructing them that absolute exemption was to be granted in cases where the tribunals were fully satisfied of the facts.

Before the Act was passed the Society of Friends reaffirmed its attitude to conscription in the following words:

"We regard the central conception of the Act as imperilling the liberty of the individual conscience, which is the main hope of human progress—and as entrenching more deeply that militarism from which we all desire the world to be freed. . . .

"We consider that young men do important service by going before the tribunals claiming exemption, and making clear their reasons for doing so. At the same time, we cannot admit that a human tribunal is an adequate judge of any man's conscience."

Tribunals were soon to show the truth of this last sentence. One or two instances quoted by J. W. Graham will show this: "At Oxford, the Mayor, a tradesman in High Street, had at his disposal the liberties of undergraduates plainly of a high spiritual type. He was aided by a military representative, much out of his depth, who inquired of a religious applicant whether Jesus had not said, 'An eye for an eye and a tooth for a tooth.' In reply he got half a chapter from the Sermon on the Mount read to him. The same gentleman also thought that Tolstoy was the name of a place. Such were the War Office ethical experts.

"Scripture was oddly used at times. A military representative at Manchester asked a man if he believed in the words, 'The meek shall inherit the earth.' 'But,' he went on, 'how can they inherit it without anybody to fight for them?' At a tribunal near London a young man began to explain the meaning of a certain passage 'in the Greek.' 'Greek,' shouted the Chairman, 'you don't mean to tell me that Jesus Christ spoke Greek. He was British to the backbone!' Beside this, the Chairman who thought minesweeping was sweeping dust out of coal mines was only harmlessly ignorant of things outside his range. At Holborn, a member of the tribunal asked a man, 'Do you ever wash yourself? You don't look it. Yours is a case of an unhealthy mind in an unwholesome body.' At Shaw, in Lancashire, a member of a body bidden by the Government to be impartial and tolerant, said, 'You are exploiting God to save your own skin. You are nothing but a shivering mass of unwholesome fat.' This was addressed to a man of high scientific attainments, employed in research under the Manchester Corporation, and asked by the British Association to join one of its Research Committees. A master at Harrow, whom I knew well, was told he ought to be put across someone's knee and spanked. Such is the voice of a little brief authority." It is to be hoped that later tribunals with these examples before them will guard against allowing their own proceedings to drop to the same low level under pressure of mass hysteria in moments of crisis.

Tribunal after tribunal refused to grant absolute exemption and stated that they had no power to do so. Applicants were bullied and browbeaten and in many cases no attempt was made to consider the applications judicially.

As the war proceeded and the war fever mounted, so the Government increased its hostility to the conscientious objectors. There began the attempt of the army to break their consciences by force. Some 5,970 C.O.s altogether were court-martialled for refusing to obey military orders. It is not possible in the space available here to give more than one or two examples of what took place. Those who would know more about the Military Service Acts and conscientious objectors are referred to *Troublesome People*, published by the No-Conscription Fellowship at the close of the 1914 war. Here an account will be read of some thirty C.O.s who were taken to France and sentenced to death in defiance of Government pledges. They were traced through

64

the ingenuity of the N.C.F. and at the last moment their sentences were commuted to penal servitude.

J. W. Graham quotes the following letter[1] from the guard-room at Pontefract as typical of military methods:

"April 4, 1916.

"DEAR COMRADES,

"Still alive and fighting. Have been forcibly examined but have refused any payment or to sign any papers, and have refused to don the uniform about half a dozen times. Consequently I am still in civilians; but they are going to use force in the end. They have tried all means to induce me to wear the uniform— threats, demands, requests, entreaties, and, worst of all, have impressed upon me the absolute insignificance of one individual in a modern army. The officers told me that, having been handed over by the country to the Army authorities they could do just as they liked with me. It is not until then that one realizes the worst of conscription. When I refused to be examined they told me it would be of no avail, since they could tame lions in the Army. I replied that they could perhaps make lions tame, but they could never make lambs fierce! They have offered to forgive my past offences if I will start and be a soldier from this moment, and thus save themselves a great deal of trouble and myself a good deal of suffering, they say. I expect I shall get about two years in a military prison, probably as an example. . . . Numerous kindly intentioned officers have endeavoured to persuade me to accept the inevitable, and give up acting the goat. But when a man is prepared to give his life for his ideals, surely veiled threats or suffering will not alter his decision."

A more extreme, and not so common, case of brutality in military prisons is the following example:[2] "On Monday morning, May 7, 1917, the breaking-in processes were begun on Gray by the bombing officer, who used his powers of per-

[1] *The Tribunal*, May 11, 1916. Letter from F. Beaumont.
[2] *Conscription and Conscience*, pp. 143–4.

suasion by means of more or less gentle ankle-tapping to bring him to attention. Then, on Gray's refusal to salute, he foamed at the mouth, and gave vent to terrible language. Subsequently he threw a live Mills-bomb at his feet, after removing the pin and failing to persuade Gray to throw it when ordered. Gray stood perfectly calm and still when the bomb was hissing at his feet, and the officer who threw it had to run for cover. The officer then wanted to shake hands with Gray, saying, 'Your —— guts are in the right place, anyhow,' but Gray declined.

"After dinner there was a repetition. Tuesday morning, May 8th, Gray was introduced to the physical training staff and Lieutenant ——. Here abuse and persuasion were blended, and on Gray's refusing to obey, his tunic was removed, shirt neck opened, puttee tied round his waist in lieu of a belt. Orders were then given, all of which he refused to obey, and was knocked into the various positions each time. The sergeant burst his mouth with a heavy blow. He was threatened with a ducking in the pond. Next day there was a repetition, and he had to endure a very long stand in the position referred to, facing a bitterly cold wind (the camp is a very exposed one), interluded with threats hurled at him by the company sergeant-major, who had a valise filled with stones, which Gray was to be made to carry as a pack under forced marching. Under these accumulated threats Gray broke down for the first time, the ordeal being beyond physical endurance. Many other and very varied acts of brutality were committed which can all be proved by eye-witnesses, such as the use of soft soap rubbed over the head and face by N.C.O.s and others, who manifested unmitigated delight in exercising their brutality."

So bad did the treatment of objectors in military prisons become that even the conscience of the Government was aroused and an order was issued in May, 1916, that all objectors were to be sent after court martial to civil prisons. In September the War Office issued an order to try to restrain brutal and illegal acts on the part of officers.

Clifford Allen in his presidential address in April, 1916, to the First Conference of the No-Conscription Fellowship restated the case for freedom of conscience in the following words:

"The members of the No-Conscription Fellowship base their fundamental objection to conscription on this ground; that whatever else a State may or may not do, whatever infringement of individual liberty a State may or may not effect, there is one interference with individual judgment that no State in the world has any sanction to enforce—that is, to tamper with the unfettered free right of every man to decide for himself the issue of life and death. We contend that the individual conscience alone must decide whether a man will inflict death upon other people in time of war, and that however far the State may impose its commands upon the will of the community, the right of private judgment in this particular must be left to the individual, since human personality is a thing which must be held as sacred. Upon that we have built up our organization."

This organization which carried on a large part of the struggle from 1914 to 1918 for freedom of conscience, was one of the most remarkable societies which has ever existed. Some of its history recalls vividly the persecution of opinion in the late eighteenth and early nineteenth centuries. It was never suppressed entirely by the Government. Member after member of its Executive Committee was sent to prison. As fast as one vanished, so another took his place.

At the prosecution of some of the Committee of the N.C.F., Mr. Bodkin, the Public Prosecutor, had said: "War would become impossible if all men were to have the view that war was wrong." A journalist was subsequently prosecuted for displaying a poster issued by the N.C.F. with only these words on it! Attempt after attempt was made to suppress the printing of their paper *The Tribunal*. The printers' office was raided and the machinery seized, so a secret printing press, which had been bought some time before, was used. Although the Fellowship's Office was watched continually by the police they never managed to find where it was printed. Never did the paper fail to appear. Thus did the N.C.F. carry on the twin struggle for freedom of conscience and liberty of opinion.

The Military Service Acts ceased to operate at the end of the war, but the last conscientious objector was not released until July, 1919. The final vindictive action against the objectors was the provision made whereby they were not allowed to vote for five years after the war. In opposing this provision Lord Hugh Cecil said in a powerful speech: "I am most anxious that this country should maintain the proposition that there is a higher law, that we view with admiration any appeal to that higher law and that we will not listen to the doctrine that the State's interest is to be supreme, but, on the contrary, that we will make our authority conform to the high standard and keep the State within its proper function, and within its proper scope.

"Belief in the State cannot help us to bear the sufferings or control the passions of war. It is a barren faith, as well as a degrading faith. It does but encumber us and shut out from us that higher world in which we ought to live."

The No-Conscription Fellowship dissolved itself in November, 1919, as it felt that the purpose for which it was formed had come to an end. In reviewing the sequel one may perhaps regret that it did not remain in existence as an organization for defending liberty and so ease the task of the conscientious objectors of 1939 and 1940.

Chapter 5

BETWEEN TWO WARS

*Prisoner, tell me who was it that wrought this unbreakable
chain? "It was I," said the prisoner, "who forged this chain
very carefully. I thought my invincible power would hold
the world captive, leaving me in a freedom undisturbed.
Thus night and day I worked at the chain with huge fires
and cruel hard strokes. When at last the work was done
and the links were complete and unbreakable, I found that
it held me in its grip."* RABINDRANATH TAGORE

The war legislation came to an end with the termination of the
War, but liberty was not restored to her old place of honour.
Instead there began the process of erosion which continued
until the next war.

The attacks came from three sides—from Acts of Parliament,
from decisions of the Law Courts and from administrative
actions of the executive. Only a short summary of these attacks
can be given here, but further reference may be made to *Civil
Liberties*,[1] by W. H. Thompson, and to the various publications
of the National Council for Civil Liberties.[2] The statutory attacks
upon liberty demand our first attention. The effect of the Emergency Powers Act, 1920, still in force, is to enable the Government to declare a state of emergency in any large-scale industrial
dispute. The only restrictions imposed on the Government by
this Act are that they may not make regulations imposing compulsory military service or industrial conscription or make it an
offence to take part in a strike or peacefully to persuade others
to take part in a strike, nor can they suspend Habeas Corpus or

[1] Victor Gollancz, 1934.   [2] 37, Gt. James's Street, W.C.1.

alter criminal procedure or impose a higher penalty than that of a fine of £100 and/or three months' imprisonment. The most famous occasion on which this Act was used was that of the General Strike of 1926, when a regulation was made providing the penalty of imprisonment for doing any act calculated to cause disaffection amongst the civil population. W. H. Thompson comments that magistrates tended to read the word "disaffection" as though it was "dis-satisfaction with the government." For saying "The Government is out to crush the workers," a member of the Labour Party received two months' imprisonment, although, after the strike, this sentence was set aside on appeal.

At the same time was passed the Official Secrets Act, 1920, which the Attorney-General of that time told the House of Commons was intended to deal with spying and attempts at spying only. The majority of Members of Parliament with their characteristic credulity believed him. In 1938 the case of a Stockport journalist came before Lord Hewart, Lord Chief Justice of England, who had been that Attorney-General in 1920. The journalist was held by Lord Hewart and the other judges to be properly convicted of an offence under this Act for refusing to tell the police where he had obtained a police circular. The offence, it may be noted, had nothing whatever to do with spying. The statement made to the House of Commons by the Attorney-General had proved, as in other cases, to be an assurance of no value at all. The journalist was convicted under a section of this Act of 1920, which made it a criminal offence not to reply to questions put by the police relating to any suspected offence under these Acts. Even Members of Parliament were not safe. It will be remembered that Mr. Sandys was threatened by the Attorney-General with a prosecution under the Official Secrets Acts for refusing to disclose, in 1939, where he obtained certain information. When this happened, Parliament took up the question vigorously, and as a result of the report of the Committee on Privileges it is unlikely that such an attempt will again be made.

n the same year an Act was passed permitting compulsory questioning only in cases of espionage.

The next Act to attack liberty was passed in 1927—the Trade Disputes and Trade Unions Act—after the General Strike. This Act interfered with the liberty of organization of the working classes. Generally speaking it made a sympathetic strike illegal, restricted peaceful picketing and prohibited Civil Service unions from having any association with outside bodies, such as the Trade Union Congress.

In 1934 came the Incitement to Disaffection Act, passed ostensibly to deal with persons who endeavoured to encourage sailors, soldiers and airmen to disobey orders. The Act was not necessary as, under an Act of 1797, this offence was already punishable with penal servitude for life; but the lower penalties provided by this Act of 1934 meant that the offence could be tried before magistrates; so that if there were many offenders they could easily be dealt with. Was the Act passed in order to deal with pacifists, or people who might be opposing the Government's war policy? It is significant that it was made a criminal offence to be in possession of literature, the distribution of which would amount to incitement of disaffection amongst the Forces, if a person had it in his possession with intent to distribute it to them. "Intention" will always be inferred from the surrounding circumstances. In time of war and popular emotion it is not difficult, whatever the evidence, to persuade a bench of magistrates that a pacifist has this intention. It is also significant that the scope of this Act has been in effect very considerably extended by Defence Regulation 39A.

The last attack upon civil liberty by Act of Parliament came with the Public Order Act of 1936. This Act was passed ostensibly to deal with Mosley and his Fascists. The House of Commons was told, and believed (once again!) that further powers were needed to suppress their riotous conduct. This view was not correct. The Act placed (*inter alia*) restrictions on the holding of public processions. But perhaps the most dangerous part of it was clause 5, which runs as follows: "Any person who in any public place or at any public meeting uses threatening abusive or insulting words or behaviour with intent to provoke a breach of the Peace, or whereby a breach of the peace is likely to be occasioned shall be guilty of an offence." The penalty is imprisonment for not more than three months and/or a fine not exceeding £50. No breach of the peace need have taken place. One of the first cases in which this Act was used was in the Harworth Colliery Dispute of 1937.

Charges of "insulting words and behaviour" under this or earlier Acts include the following: a newspaper seller of the *Daily Worker* calling out his newspaper placard "Andre executed by Nazis"; a man during a demonstration calling out "Give us bread"; a pacifist putting a peace poster on a fence near the Hendon Air Display.

By 1939 it was clear that any public political activity to which the police took exception would be charged as insulting words or behaviour, and convictions in many courts became nearly automatic. This position remains unchanged.

Not only by statute but by decisions of the Law Courts has liberty been curtailed since 1918. Such decisions have limited the right of meeting in the highway. It has been held that the police can stop any outdoor meeting if they reasonably apprehend a breach of the peace; but there is no way of finding out what are the exact contents of the policeman's mind, when he says he reasonably apprehends this. So if a speaker at a public meeting in the open air refuses to close the meeting when ordered to do so by the police, he is liable to be charged with obstructing the police in the execution of their duty if they reasonably apprehend a breach of the peace. Thus the right to hold open-air meetings had gone before the outbreak of the present war and they, in effect, could be prevented whenever the authorities wished.

The decision extending the right of search has already been referred to on page 42.

Another legal decision has established that the police have a right to enter a private meeting, if they consider it likely that a crime will be committed or that a breach of the peace will occur if they are not present. In 1934 when Mosley held a meeting at Olympia the police refused to enter it on the ground that they had no power to do so, but when a meeting was held in South Wales to protest against the Incitement to Disaffection Bill, the Law Courts held they had this power. This power is in part confirmed by the Public Order Act, 1936.

When the authorities are not satisfied with the further powers conferred on them by statute and common law, there exist earlier Statutes and legal weapons which can be used. Even an Act of Edward III's reign has been dragged out on occasion. Some years ago Tom Mann and another, who were organizing a meeting of the unemployed in Trafalgar Square, were summoned under this Act, because, as the prosecution said, it was feared that they would commit a crime by holding an illegal meeting. The magistrate required them to be bound over to keep the peace, and when they refused they were sent to prison for two months although they had not been charged with any criminal offence. The power to bind persons over who have not committed any criminal offence is power which may well be used to suppress opposition to the Government.

It is not possible to do more than mention some of the other powers which the State has. There is the offence of sedition or seditious libel, which may be defined as:

All practices, short of treason, which have for their object:

1. To excite discontent or dissatisfaction;
2. To excite ill will between different classes of the King's subjects;
3. To create public disturbance or lead to a civil war;
4. To bring into hatred the Sovereign, Government, laws, or Constitution of the Realm.[1]

[1] Garcia's *Criminal Law and Pleadings* (Sweet & Maxwell).

There is the offence of unlawful assembly which consists, *inter alia*, of three or more persons assembling for any purpose in such a manner so as to cause reasonable persons to fear a breach of the peace.

There is the Seditious Meetings Act, 1817, which makes it illegal for more than fifty persons to meet in the open air within one mile of the Houses of Parliament for the purpose of considering any petition to Parliament or the King at a time when Parliament is sitting. There is the Act of 1661 which makes it illegal for more than ten persons at any time to go to Parliament with a Petition.

There is the offence of blasphemy already dealt with and there is the offence of obscene libel.

In addition to specific statutes and judicial decisions, civil rights have frequently been curtailed—particularly since 1918—by social legislation; but we cannot extend this chapter by delving into the subtleties of this third method of restricting human freedom.

Chapter 6

THE GROWTH OF BUREAUCRACY

"Writers on the Constitution have for a long time taught that its two leading features are the Sovereignty of Parliament and the Rule of Law. To tamper with either of them was, it might be thought, a sufficiently serious undertaking. But how far more attractive to the ingenious and adventurous mind to employ the one to defeat the other, and to establish a despotism on the ruins of both! It is manifestly easy to point a superficial contrast between what was done or attempted in the days of our least wise kings and what is being done or attempted to-day. In those days the method was to defy Parliament—and it failed. In these days the method is to cajole, to coerce, and to use Parliament—and it is strangely successful. The old despotism, which was defeated, offered Parliament a challenge. The new despotism, which is not yet defeated, gives Parliament an anaesthetic. The strategy is different, but the goal is the same. It is to subordinate Parliament, to evade the Courts, and to render the will, or the caprice, of the Executive unfettered and supreme."

The increasing scope and complexity of modern legislation has led Parliament more and more to delegate its power of making laws to Government departments, by granting them power to legislate by rule and order. This is an inevitable consequence of modern conditions, and has been particularly noticeable since 1918. It must be accepted so long as the delegated power is confined to details and subjected to proper control.

Neither of these conditions has in fact been observed and public concern as to the manner in which these rules, regulations and orders were being made was reflected in a book by the Lord Chief Justice entitled *The New Despotism* (from which the extract

75

at the opening of this chapter is taken), and culminated in the setting up of the Committee on Ministers' Powers which reported in 1932. This Committee is generally known as "The Donoughmore Committee."

Their report contained a long series of recommendations which had the following objects:

1. *The provision of adequate control of Ministerial Orders by the Courts of Law.*—In the past a citizen has always had the safeguard that if aggrieved he could go to the Courts, and if they found that the Minister had exceeded the powers conferred on him by Parliament they would quash the Order. In recent years, however, there has been inserted in many statutes a clause deliberately designed to deprive the citizen of his right to challenge the validity of orders or regulations.

The Committee in this connection recommended: (*a*) that the use of clauses designed to exclude the jurisdiction of the Courts should be abandoned in all but exceptional cases;

(*b*) that where exceptional cases are considered necessary it should be clearly stated that it is the intention to make the exclusion, and a period of three months and preferably six months should be allowed in which the orders can be challenged in the Courts;

(*c*) that Acts of Parliament should not use vague language so that it is uncertain as to whether or not a person can contest his rights in the Law Courts.

2. *The Abolition of wide Ministerial Powers*, such as (to take the extreme case) the so-called "Henry VIII Clause," which confers power on a Minister to modify the provisions of former Acts of Parliament. Generally speaking Acts of Parliament should only be amended by Parliament itself.

3. *Proper publicity and notice of all proposed rules and regulations.* Of recent years there has been a tendency towards secrecy and rush.

4. *Adequate supervision by Parliament.*—The Donoughmore Committee recommended that each House of Parliament should

set up a small Committee to consider (*a*) all Bills which confer powers on Ministers to make rules, and (*b*) all regulations made under Acts of Parliament.

Not only was no attempt made to carry out these recommendations of the Donoughmore Committee, but many provisions of Acts of Parliament, passed since 1932, deliberately flouted them. For instance the Agricultural Marketing Act, 1933, only allowed twenty-eight days in which an order made under it could be challenged in the Courts. Another instance was contained in the Military Training Act, 1939. The old "Henry VIII clause" only gave the Minister power to modify earlier Acts of Parliament so far as might be necessary to bring the enacting statute into force, but there was no such limit under the Military Training Act. An Order-in-Council under that Act might be made modifying any other statute. So, under the pretext that it was necessary for carrying out the provisions of the Military Training Act, an Order in Council could have been made suspending or repealing Magna Carta, the Habeas Corpus Acts and other statutes which safeguard liberty.

Moreover, further abuses developed. When, in the past, Acts of Parliament have conferred upon departments the power to make regulations, the Acts themselves have laid down the maximum penalty for a breach of such Regulations. In 1934 the Board of Trade introduced a Bill setting up a system of clearing houses to deal with frozen debts. By its terms, the Board was empowered to make an Order for certain purposes, and it was laid down that the Order itself should prescribe the penalty for a breach of the Order; that is to say, the Board of Trade might have prescribed the death penalty had it thought fit, for an offence under this particular Act. There were immediate protests, one is glad to note, in the House of Commons. The Solicitor-General of the day admitted that he could furnish no precedent for a proposal of this kind, and ultimately, in deference to the general feeling of the House, the Government gave way and agreed to insert a maximum monetary penalty. Two years later the same Department (i.e. the Board of Trade) was responsible for a Bill dealing with merchant shipping in Spanish waters. Substantially the same proposal was introduced, namely that no maximum penalty was exacted for a breach of the Act. On this occasion, in spite of protests from the Liberal Opposition and from Sir Stafford Cripps, it passed into law. This was followed by other Acts, e.g. the Military Training Act, 1939, giving the Minister power to decide what punishment should be inflicted for a breach of regulations he had power to make.

Not only was there a tendency throughout this period for Parliament to delegate its powers to Government departments, but Parliament created Government bodies which were placed outside its immediate control. The Assistance Board is a case in point. This body is not represented by a responsible Minister in Parliament, and its administration cannot be criticized in the way, for example, that of the Post Office can be. Its officials are not necessarily civil servants whose appointment and remuneration is scrutinized in the public interest by the Public Accounts Committee of the House of Commons. In some cases (e.g. the B.B.C.) the officials spend large sums of public money without having to submit their accounts to that Committee.

Delegated powers of legislation are exceptionally dangerous in the hands of these bodies. Take the case of the Assistance Board set up in 1934. It is not answerable to the Minister of Labour and over it, therefore, Parliament can exercise no continuous supervision. The Board has power to make regulations governing the administration of the means test, but the question as to whether, and if so when, new regulations are necessary is entirely one for the Board. The Minister may indeed amend the Board's draft regulations before presenting them to Parliament, but he has no power to order when new regulations should be made.

Further, there is the method so frequently adopted nowadays of embodying important measures in orders or regulations which the two Houses of Parliament may accept or reject, but cannot amend. The regulations of the Assistance Board are typical. Although they affect hundreds of thousands of households and are of infinitely greater importance than many Bills that come before the House of Commons, the House is powerless to alter a single word unless they reject the whole set. The same criticism applied to the Agricultural Marketing Schemes which affected the livelihoods of large numbers of citizens. The position was the same under the Military Training Act. In one day four orders which vitally affected the civil rights of militia-men with regard to such matters as rent and hire purchase agreements were passed by Parliament. Not one amendment could be made.

It is inevitable that under modern conditions of extended social services, town planning, and regulation of industry and agriculture, Government departments besides possessing delegated powers of legislation should have to decide individual cases affecting the rights and property of citizens. For example, the Ministry of Pensions decides cases in which it is claimed that a war widow's pension ought to be stopped, and the Ministry of Health whether certain houses should be condemned as a slum area. It is often necessary for these powers of adjudication to be given to Ministers and departments, but if the citizen is to be secure from arbitrary acts of the Executive, he must have his rights decided by a body of persons, who are not directly interested in the result, who have many years of training and practice by which they arrive at their judgments and discover the principles involved, and all classes of the community must be equal before the law. It may be agreed that it is necessary for the administration of many laws dealing with social conditions that they should not be administered by the ordinary Courts of Law, since it is much simpler, quicker and cheaper for them to to be dealt with by special tribunals, but such tribunals must act in accordance with commonly accepted principles of justice. It is, for instance, a principle of law that a man should not be judge in his own cause, but departments are more often than not interested in the disputes which arise out of their administration. In pension cases the officials of the department concerned (whose real master is the Treasury) are interested in the "economy" involved in the possible saving of the pensions. In all such cases it is only fair that the dispute should be referred to a really independent tribunal.

The secrecy of these administrative tribunals is to be deplored. Appeals may be made to the Minister and dismissed and the appellant may never know the grounds on which the appeal was decided. The decisions of these tribunals which deal with principle should always—as is sometimes now the case—be published and a man should be entitled to state his case properly before the tribunal. It has often been said that it is important that justice should not only be done but appear to be done. Until these reforms are carried out it will not always be apparent.

Another injustice was the denial of legal representation before bodies such as the Appeal Tribunals set up under the Unemployment Assistance Act, 1934, and the Courts of Referees and the Umpire under the Unemployment Insurance scheme. Many people are unable to state their case logically and coherently, but unless they belong to a trade union when their union representative may appear for them before the Courts of Referees or Umpires, they may not be represented, e.g. by a barrister or solicitor. The author is fully aware of the deficiencies of the English legal profession, but it is the injustice of denying men the right to employ skilled advocates against which he is protesting. If it is suggested that not all men could afford advocates it may be pointed out that defects in the organization of the legal system of this country are not good reasons for denying an elementary right to disputants, and that as long as a system of society based on wealth and privileges exists this argument will apply in every department of life. Moreover, many of these tribunals deal with questions of law. The Umpire under the Unemployment Insurance Acts has decided hundreds of cases, but it is unlikely that they will be familiar to a person applying for benefit, although no doubt the officials will be fully cognisant of these. In a recent case where a conscientious objector had left his work for conscientious reasons, he was denied benefit on the ground that he was not sincere. He had no right of legal assistance and finally had his appeal dismissed by the Umpire without having any chance to argue it, although in the meantime he had been given unconditional exemption by the tribunal.

In the late 'thirties the manner in which Marketing Boards imposed penalties met with much criticism. For the first time in English history, power had been given to bodies elected by restricted groups to inflict penalties instead of such power being vested in the ordinary criminal courts. Another Government committee recommended that penalties or fines by such bodies should only be imposed by a special tribunal, with a lawyer as chairman, and that there should be a right of appeal to an independent arbitrator. The carrying out of these recommendations would have removed the reproach that the Marketing Boards were acting as judges in their own causes. Moreover, it is worth while considering if similar provisions should not be applied to voluntary price fixing associations as well.

The powers of Government Departments are enhanced by the legal principle that the Crown cannot be sued for a wrong. A practical example will make the matter clearer. If a pedestrian is knocked down by a Post Office van, his only practicable course is to sue the driver of the van and not the Postmaster-General to whom the Crown's privileges extend. It is true that the Postmaster-General usually provides legal assistance for the driver and pays any damages which may be awarded against him, but it is not satisfactory that a person's right against a Government department should depend on the department's good grace. The law on this matter is founded on ancient considerations which no longer hold good. If local authorities as large and important as the London County Council can do without this archaic privilege, there is no reason why Government departments should continue to enjoy it.

Furthermore, when the Crown sues a citizen in certain criminal and in tax cases it has special privileges which very seriously handicap the defendant. In an action against a Government department it is often necessary to use an ancient and archaic form of procedure known as Petition of Right. The Attorney-General's consent is necessary to this and as an officer of the Crown he may not always be impartial. Finally the rule that the Crown is not bound by an Act of Parliament unless this is expressly laid down often creates much hardship.

The Crown's position in law cases was considered by a Committee which was first appointed in 1921. In 1927 the Committee presented a Draft Bill, called the Crown Proceedings Bill, which would have put Government departments and the Crown in the same position as an ordinary litigant, and taken away from them these archaic and special privileges and remedies which are unsuited to modern conditions and fulfil no purpose but that of bolstering up bureaucracy. This Committee's Report included a draft bill to abolish these unnecessary privileges and rights of the Crown, but owing, it may be, to interested opposition the Bill never passed into law.

It should by now be clear that by statutory changes, by decisions in the Courts and by a great increase of bureaucratic power civil liberty had been steadily diminishing from 1919 to the summer of 1939.

Chapter 7

FREEDOM NOW

Liberty, let others despair of you—I never despair of you.
Is the house shut? is the master away?
Nevertheless, be ready, be not weary of watching,
He will soon return, his messengers come anon.

WALT WHITMAN

On August 24, 1939, the Emergency Powers (Defence) Act was passed into law. The only Members of Parliament who voted against this Act were: T. Edmund Harvey, George Lansbury, Cecil H. Wilson, James Maxton, Campbell Stephen and John McGovern. Attempts were made to amend it during its passage through the House of Commons, but these were not successful, and the Bill passed into law as introduced. Many Members of Parliament, whose names one had been accustomed to see recorded in Hansard as defenders of civil liberty in the House, were conspicuous by their absence from the discussion of this Bill. Particular tribute, however, should be paid to Mr. T. Edmund Harvey, who made efforts to improve it. The only things the Government might not do under this Act were to impose compulsory military service or industrial conscription or provide for the trial of civilians by military law. Subject to these restrictions such defence regulations might be made "as appeared to be necessary or expedient for securing the public safety, the defence of the realm, the maintenance of public order and the efficient prosecution of any war in which His Majesty may be engaged, and for maintaining supplies and services essential to the life of the community." Further powers are conferred by the Emergency Powers (Defence) Act, 1940, which provides that, notwithstanding anything in the earlier Act, the Government shall have power "to make such Defence Regulations making provision for requiring persons to place themselves, their services, and their property at the disposal of His Majesty, as appear to him to be necessary or expedient for securing the public safety, the defence of the Realm, the maintenance of public order, or the efficient prosecution of any war in which His Majesty may be engaged, or for maintaining supplies or services essential to the life of the community."

The restriction remaining on the Government's powers is that relating to the trial of civilians by court martial. Here we must note the Emergency Powers (Defence) Act passed in August 1940. The effect of this Act is that wherever the military situation makes it necessary, defence regulations may be made providing for the apprehension and punishment and trial of offenders before such courts and with such procedure as may be specified. Reviews of decisions of these Courts must be made by a Tribunal composed of three persons who have held high judicial office in all cases involving death, and in other cases as may be provided by regulations. Parliament in its discussions on this Act, and the amendments made to it, certainly showed its independence and understanding of the necessity of liberty. The reader may be reminded of the criticism invoked by the regulations under D.O.R.A. providing for the trial of certain offences by court martial. The Government has wider powers than the Executive has had ever before in English history. The dictatorial powers are in law almost complete.

Without any need to seek the consent of Parliament, there is power under these Acts to detain persons without trial, to prohibit peace and political meetings, to forbid a person from entering a particular area, to dissolve societies and parties, to prohibit or censor any newspaper, pamphlet or book, and to inflict the death penalty for new or existing offences.[1] In short

[1] Since this essay was written two defence regulations providing the death penalty as a punishment for two new offences have been issued viz. forcing a safeguard (i.e. a military cordon or sentry) and looting property in an area subject to enemy attack.

here is power to destroy every one of those liberties of the subject which have been painfully built up from generation to generation.

Moreover, any Act of Parliament can be suspended or amended.

While the first Act was passing through Parliament, there was some discussion as to whether it gave power to amend the Emergency Powers (Defence) Act itself. The Attorney-General said that it did not, but this statement has been doubted by some lawyers, and if the matter comes before the courts a general experience of what happens to liberty before the law courts in time of war does not lead one to suppose that it will be victorious.

These powers have not so far been exercised to their full extent. The Defence Regulations which were made on September 1st were, as a result of a debate in Parliament towards the end of October, 1939, amended at the end of November, and it was hoped that some of the dangers to liberty had been removed. Further regulations inimical to liberty have, however, since been made.

It may be noted that many of the regulations offer a close resemblance to regulations issued under the old Defence of the Realm Acts.

The first thing to notice is that the Home Secretary was given absolute power to detain persons whom he believed to be of hostile origin or associations, or to have been engaged in acts prejudicial to the public safety or the defence of the realm, in such places and under such conditions as he might determine. In fact the Habeas Corpus Acts, one of the oldest safeguards of the subject against illegal imprisonment, have been, in this regard, suspended. The Home Secretary might act on mere suspicion. Advisory Committees are set up to hear appeals against an order of detention, but he may entirely disregard their advice, and no barrister or solicitor may represent the internee before the committee. Persons may be interned who are British subjects. The Courts of Law have no power to interfere when a person is thus detained.

85

This Regulation (18B) was amended by providing that the Home Secretary must have "reasonable cause" before interning any person. It has been contended that the introduction of these words "reasonable cause" restores the right of the law court to enquire if it is reasonable for the Home Secretary to detain a person, but this view is not correct.

Other amendments to this regulation provided that the Home Secretary is to report monthly to Parliament any case in which he does not follow the advice of the Advisory Committee. This regulation was amended in May, 1940, by giving the Home Secretary power to intern persons whom he suspected of being members of an organization subject to foreign influence or control or which has persons in control who have or have had associations with persons concerned in the government of or sympathies with the system of government of any power with which the country is at war. Regulation 18BB authorizes a Regional Commissioner to detain any person for the reasons mentioned in 18B while the Home Secretary considers if he should be incarcerated under an order of detention.

An order of detention may be suspended on conditions made by the Home Secretary prohibiting or restricting the possession or use of any specified articles; restricting the prospective internee in his employment, in his association or communication with other persons. Another regulation gives the Home Secretary power to make an order controlling a person's movements and place of residence, if he is satisfied that it is necessary to do so in order to prevent the person acting in any manner prejudicial to the public safety or defence of the realm.

Regulation 39A, in effect, extends the Incitement to Disaffection Act, 1934. This makes it an offence to endeavour to seduce from their duties persons in His Majesty's Service, or engaged under any public authority in the performance of functions in connection with the defence of the realm or the securing of the public safety, or to cause among such persons disaffection likely to lead to breaches of their duties. This egulation not only makes the presence of such persons at their meetings dangerous for pacifist speakers, but it might make it an offence for a person to suggest to an employee engaged on war work that he is not properly treated by his employers.

A new regulation was made in May, 1940, which provides that it is a criminal offence to incite persons, who are or may become liable under the National Service (Armed Forces) Act, 1939, to be called up for service, to evade any duties or liabilities which they are or may become liable to perform or discharge under that Act. The effect of this is that any propaganda directed towards men under forty-one with a view to persuading them that they should register as conscientious objectors is illegal; any pacifist propaganda or activity among non-pacifists which would be likely to produce the same result is illegal; and any pacifist propaganda or work amongst men of military age who are not declared pacifists and conscientious objectors may be illegal. It is even illegal for a parent to urge his son of adolescent years to become a conscientious objector. The same regulation makes it illegal to endeavour to incite persons not to join the armed forces voluntarily, or in any civil defence organization; or to endeavour to prejudice the training, discipline or administration of the forces or any such organization. It is obvious that this might be used to prevent trade union activity amongst A.R.P. workers.

A similar provision to one in the 1934 Act exists as to the possession of literature, but under the wide scope of these regulations the power taken is even more dangerous.

Regulation 39B as originally drafted could have been used to suppress any propaganda which the Government disliked. It provided that no person might endeavour, whether orally or otherwise, to influence public opinion—or the opinion of any section of the public—in a manner likely to be prejudicial to (a) the defence of the realm or (b) the efficient prosecution of war. It was also made a criminal offence to do any act, or have any article in one's possession, with the view to influencing persons in the manner described. The word "article" included a book, paper and pamphlet.

This regulation was substantially amended, so that it is now only an offence to endeavour by means of any false statement, false document, or false report to influence public opinion in the manner described.

Further regulations made in May, 1940, give the Home Secretary power to serve a notice in writing on any person who has spoken words or written anything which the Home Secretary thinks is calculated to foment opposition to the waging of the war to a successful conclusion, if he thinks "serious mischief" might be caused by any further activity on the same lines. If, after receipt of this notice, the person warned speaks any words or writes anything (whether or not similar to that for which the warning was given) which is calculated to foment opposition to victory, or assists any other person to do the same, he can be charged at the Assizes or the Old Bailey and, if found guilty, may be sent to penal servitude for not more than seven years and/or fined £500. It is also illegal after such warning has been given to be in possession of literature with the intention of committing such an offence. Provision is also made for serving a notice on the manager of any organization engaged in this activity which is described as "corruption of public morale." If such notice is disregarded, any person taking part in the management or control of the organization or society can be prosecuted. This regulation might even make illegal the advocacy of a peace by negotiation. The court has no power to investigate as to whether a warning has been properly given.

If the Home Secretary thinks that any printing apparatus has been used to produce a document for which a person has been convicted under these new Regulations, or under the earlier Regulations dealing with propaganda and incitement to disaffection (39A and 39B), he may prohibit its use until the matter has been brought before the High Court. The Court may allow the printing to continue either unconditionally if the use of the printing press was due to a mistake, or subject to conditions, or may order the printing machinery to be destroyed or forfeited.

Another regulation provides that the Home Secretary may forbid the printing, publication and distribution of any newspaper which is, in his opinion, calculated to foment opposition to the prosecution of the war to a successful conclusion, and there are powers of dealing with printing presses similar to those mentioned in the last paragraph, but no order declaring a newspaper to be illegal need have been made for a printing press to be seized. It is sufficient for the printer to have been habitually printing any newspaper which is consistently undermining "the will to victory." It is made illegal to re-start a suppressed newspaper under any other name, but in any event it would be impossible as the Minister of Supply has forbidden the printing or publication of any newspaper, magazine or other periodical that was not published at any time before August, 1940.

Any person who publishes any report or statement relating to matters connected with the war which is likely to cause alarm or despondency is liable to a fine of £50 and/or imprisonment of one month. It is a good defence for the person charged to prove:

(a) That he had reasonable cause to believe that the report or statement was true; and

(b) That the publication thereof was not malicious and ought fairly to be excused.

Regulation 39E, as originally drafted, provided that the Home Secretary, or any Mayor, Chief Constable or Magistrate, to whom the power was delegated, might prohibit any meeting which he thought would be likely to cause serious public disorder or to promote disaffection. The power to delegate was withdrawn when the regulation was amended, but the same effect is arrived at by the power of any Chief Officer of Police to restrict or prohibit assemblies and the use of premises as a place of public resort on the grounds of safety. If an order prohibiting a public meeting is made under this power, it is not possible to enquire what was really in the Chief Constable's mind.

The astonishing powers of search given to the police by the Defence Regulations have already been referred to in Chapter 3. It must, however, be emphasized that it is contrary to the principles of English liberty to put the power of authorizing a search into the hands of servants of the Executive. The power of arrest can now be exercised by any constable or member of the armed forces in the course of his duty, or person authorized by the Home Secretary, as regards any person whom he reasonably suspects of having committed an offence against the regulations. Thus a person who had accidentally left a light exposed during the "black out" could be arrested under this power. Moreover, to give such powers, however necessary in cases of espionage and similar offences, to members of the military forces is still more repugnant to English constitutional principles, particularly in political cases.

A wide power of censorship was originally conferred upon the Minister of Information, who was given power to prohibit the publication of any matters which he thought might be prejudicial to the efficient prosecution of the war. This power can now be exercised only if the publication would prejudicially affect foreign relations; but a censorship, in effect, is brought about by making it illegal to obtain, possess or publish any matter whatsoever containing information which would, or might, be directly or indirectly useful to an enemy. If the matter is submitted to, and approved by, the censorship department of the Ministry of Information before publication, this is a complete safeguard.

Regulation 18AA establishes an undesirable precedent by giving the Home Secretary power to control and wind up any organization which (a) is subject to foreign influence or control, or (b) has, or has had, persons in control of it associated with persons in the government of, or sympathetic with, the system of government of any country with which this country is at war.

90

If such organization is prohibited, it is made illegal to attend any meeting of it as a member, or contribute any money to it, and after payment of debts all its property may be forfeited to the Crown.

It is not possible to refer to all the other regulations which may be used to suppress liberty of opinion. There are regulations dealing with curfew, prohibiting the entry of persons to protected places or protected areas, power to compel information to be supplied and any articles to be produced, and so on.[1]

Another measure to which attention should be called is the Treachery Act, 1940, which imposes the death penalty for acts designed or likely to give assistance to the naval, military or air operations of the enemy, to impede such operations of the Allied armed forces or to endanger life, provided that the act is done with the intention of helping the enemy.

In connection with this Act, and all these regulations, it is important to remember that in law a man's intentions can be inferred from the reasonable and probable consequences of his acts, and for the prosecution to be successful it may not be necessary to prove the specific intention which at first sight often appears to be necessary.

It is unnecessary to make further comment on these regulations—*res ipsa loquitur*—the tendency is plain. The Government must, however, be given great credit for not having so far used them very oppressively. The activities of Fifth Columnists make it easy for ignorant Tory M.P.s and others to demand the suppression of all criticism and comment which they dislike. The danger to liberty will come—as the 1914 war showed—if reason is obscured by popular emotion, hate and hysteria—when the Government will need protecting from its friends!

Members of Parliament were grossly negligent when they allowed the first Emergency Powers (Defence) Act to pass

---

[1] Further reference may be made to *British Liberty in Danger*, by Ronald Kidd (Secretary of the National Council for Civil Liberties), Lawrence & Wishart, 5s.

without amendment. Amendments which would have substantially safeguarded liberty had been prepared, but no Member of Parliament was found to move them. No doubt in the minds of many was the thought that everything must be subordinated to the successful prosecution of the war. Labour leaders have been known to refer to principles of liberty as "Victorian." In the minds of other members of the Labour Party there may have been the thought which is often expressed by Socialists, that these powers would be useful to deal with their opponents when they came into power themselves. I suggest that these Acts still need to be amended so that, except perhaps in the case of invasion or treachery, civil liberties may not be tampered with.

The extension of the new bureaucracy (referred to in the last chapter) has proceeded apace under the powers given by the Emergency Powers (Defence) Acts and other Acts of Parliament ever since the beginning of the war. The Emergency Powers (Defence) Act, as amended, renders the continued sessions of Parliament somewhat superfluous. Almost any Act which they could pass could now be quite well enacted by a defence regulation. Presumably there is a desire to keep some democracy in being. Under the Emergency Powers (Defence) Act, industry, trade and agriculture—and labour—are controlled, apparently by ministers, but in daily practice often by men who had previously held prominent positions in the private firms of the trade. Thus it is stated in a Fabian Society pamphlet:[1] "The Bacon Controller is a representative of Marsh and Baxter; the Assistant Sugar Controller comes from Tate & Lyle; the Chairman of the Cereals Imports Committee is also the chairman of Ranks Ltd., the big milling concern; the Director of Imported Meat Supplies represents Union Cold Storage. But the most remarkable section of all is that dealing with Oils and Fats (presumably including margarine, which is to play so large a part in wartime diet), where there are eleven individuals performing administrative work. One (the worst paid, by the way)

[1] *Food in War Time*, 2d.

92

is a civil servant; one was formerly occupied running his own business; and the remaining nine were previously employed in the firm of Lever Bros and Unilever Ltd., or one of its subsidiaries."

A similar state of affairs prevails in other Controls. Further useful details will be found in *Bureaucracy Run Mad*, by Martin Abbotson.[1] The bureaucratic structure against which Lord Hewart fulminated in 1929 approaches a triumphant completion and Germany has pointed the way. If the personnel of bureaucracy ousts, as it has in Germany, the industrial and financial monopolists from their present official positions, there will be nothing to choose between the political structure of England and that of Fascist regimes.

It is true that the Government still does have Acts passed in order to make Parliament feel it retains a place in the nation's life. Regulations under pre-war Acts of Parliament are sometimes brought before it. Question time is still part of the procedure of the House. But the Executive has unlimited power under the Emergency Powers (Defence) Acts to make regulations at its own sweet will. The Factory and Coal Mines Acts can be suspended by regulation, and a number of such orders have been made. The law courts are forbidden to exercise their normal powers of supervising and controlling subordinate judicial or quasi-judicial bodies, such as the Hardship Committees or Conscientious Objectors' Tribunals. This general power of the law courts to interfere when injustice has been done by governmental bodies acting in a judicial or quasi-judicial manner, has often been a great safeguard to the liberty of the subject. For over fifty years, as described by Lord Hewart, the bureaucracy has been trying to exclude the Courts. Now it has succeeded!

There is increasing tendency to hold criminal cases in secret despite the legal maxim that "justice must not only be done but must appear to be done." Applicants for postponement of military service have their cases heard in secret, and if the

[1] Watts & Co., 1s. 3d.

decision of the Committee is unanimous they may not appeal without the leave of the Committee. But Committees do not like having their decisions appealed against. Moreover, applicants before these Committees, or before a Price Investigation Committee under the Prices of Goods Act, 1939 (i.e. the Profiteering Act), are forbidden to be represented by a solicitor or barrister unless he is a personal friend or relation. Is this because the officials who run these Committees fear that lawyers might bring out into the daylight that which now takes place in secret? Not every person is capable of putting his case in a coherent, clear and convincing manner, and it seems an injustice that he should be denied his right to employ a skilled person to present his case. Despite protests from trade associations and members of all parties, the Ministers responsible state that they are satisfied that the regulations are in the public interest.

Parliament, of course, is still useful for ventilating grievances and for publicizing injustice. But it is almost impossible to get any change against the will of the bureaucracy. As Miss Ellen Wilkinson said at the close of a debate on shipping, "Does the Minister of Shipping realize that he has not given one specific answer to any one specific question that has been put?"

Attention may also perhaps be called to the astonishing and growing practice of purporting to make changes in the law by administrative action and then validating them by Statute order or regulation at a later—sometimes much later—date. One of the most glaring examples of this was the suspension of the rationing of coal, gas and electricity in November, 1939, but the law continued to say that these articles were to be rationed until January, 1940. This procedure is becoming more frequent, and no protest is raised against it. Yet it is reminiscent of a State where a dictator says "I want the law to be" and the law accordingly is immediately "so and so." Is it by these methods that the enjoyment and the burden of life is to be spread more equally among men? Is it for this State control that men have worked and given their lives?

Chapter 8

MILITARY CONSCRIPTION

It is now necessary to consider in some detail the re-introduction in England of military conscription in 1939.

This was provided for by the Military Training Act of 1939. There was to be six months' military training of young men, and conscientious objectors to this training could register as such when the militia men registered. They then had to state their grounds for being conscientious objectors on a form of application to a local tribunal. The local tribunals which were appointed under this Act have a County Court Judge as Chairman, with four other members. These were appointed by the Minister of Labour who had to have regard to the necessity of appointing impartial persons, while one representative had to be a representative of the working classes. From the local tribunal there was an appeal to an appellate tribunal, the Chairman of which need not necessarily be a lawyer.

This method of dealing with conscientious objectors was carried over into the National Service (Armed Forces) Act, 1939, passed after the outbreak of war. This Act made all British subjects—with some exceptions—resident in Great Britain between the ages of 18 and 41 liable to compulsory military service. The classes to be called up were to be those specified by Royal Proclamation. At the time of writing Royal Proclamations cover the ages twenty to thirty-six.

It will be remembered that during the 1914 war there were some sixteen thousand conscientious objectors. At the time of writing some forty-nine thousand have registered. The number seems to be slightly decreasing as the higher age groups are reached owing, perhaps, to the war having come to our very doorsteps, and to the increasing protection of reserved occupations, and many refusing to register at all. But on a conservative estimate it is probable that there will be at least sixty thousand conscientious objectors within the age groups covered by the Act.

The tribunals under the National Service (Armed Forces) Act differ from, and are an improvement on, the Tribunals under the Military Service Act, 1916. They are appointed by the Minister of Labour who is probably more detached and impartial than local authorities who appointed the 1916 tribunals. They are smaller—a body which might consist of twenty-five members was unwieldy. Even five is probably too many, and as the experience of Magistrates Courts has shown, it tends to leave too much power and influence with the chairman. No military representative is present—the State is represented by an official of the Ministry of Labour who rarely intervenes. On some occasions the Ministry of Labour actually intervenes on behalf of the conscientious objector—particularly in cases where there has been a refusal to register and the Ministry has, under the power contained in the Act, registered him as a conscientious objector. The tribunals only deal with conscientious objectors. They generally sit in public and representatives of the Press are present, and the conscientious objectors may be legally represented. Hardship cases are dealt with by a separate committee, as mentioned on page 93.

The chairmen of the tribunals are trained lawyers and this gives sometimes an appearance of, and sometimes real, impartiality.

How have these tribunals worked? They are working out their history as this book is being written, and hence it is neither desirable, nor possible, to form any final judgments. Details of the cases before the tribunals, local and appellate, will be found in the literature issued by the various pacifist and other bodies which are opposed to conscription, but one or two judgments may be passed on their working to date. There is no doubt that they are much better—and on the whole fairer—than the

1916 tribunals. However, they have shown more clearly than ever how difficult or impossible it is for a court of tribunal to judge a man's conscience. On questions of peace and war, life or death, it is not possible to be impartial. Few members of tribunals would regard war as a good thing, but almost all of them believe this particular war to be necessary. They cannot understand the conscientious objector, whether he objects on political, religious or ethical grounds. A legal training and experience helps judges and lawyers to become impartial judges of fact, although—as has been frequently pointed out—English judges and magistrates often think they are being impartial when, in fact, they are showing, and are bound by, the limitations imposed by their environment and class. This has been illustrated in the post-1918 trials for political offences, and it is illustrated again when working-class youths come before tribunals composed for the most part of elderly and wealthy middle-class men. Often the youth can only express his abhorrence of war and his determination to take no part in it in crude and simple language. The tribunals lack the imaginative power of seeing the lad's background, upbringing and environment, and because he does not state his objections in a recognized Christian phraseology, or in precise ethical and humanistic terms, his application may be rejected. The trade unionists and others representative of the working class on the tribunals often do their best, but they lack the insight to judge the applicants properly. It is probable indeed, that the Appellate Tribunal both with its former chairman, the Rt. Hon. H. A. L. Fisher and its present chairman, Lord Fleming, has dealt with most cases much more fairly than the local tribunals.

One of the most noticeable things about these tribunals is their failure to understand the position of the absolutist—a man who refuses to accept anything except unconditional registration as a conscientious objector. On principle he denies the right of the State to conscript man, and denies its right to decide that he must be engaged in work directly or indirectly useful to the prosecution of the war. He only appears before the tribunal to testify to his belief in the freedom of conscience. The low percentage of unconditional registrations is leading many future conscientious objectors to the point where they will refuse to register when their time comes. This is a view which can be reasonably defended, yet freedom of conscience has been conceded by the State—albeit in a most imperfect form—and it is vital to preserve the concession and if possible extend it. The machinery set up therefore should be used to its fullest extent. Otherwise there is a danger that such Government and public sympathy as exists may be lost.

The conscientious objector of 1939 and 1940 has, so far, not had to undergo the privations and cruelties of his 1916 predecessor. The conscientious objectors who have first had to meet the challenge of the State at the tribunal have been those least well equipped to meet it, for not many at the ages of twenty and twenty-one can express themselves fluently, have worked out all their ideas and reasons for their beliefs and can present unshaken fronts to the tribunal. There they have to face men who are often openly hostile to their beliefs, who deride them and who ask questions which have little or no relevance to the problem of conscience.

Members of Parliament have denounced conscientious objectors views as immoral, have advocated the suppression of the Peace Pledge Union, and at least one Christian member of the tribunal is apparently of the opinion that one cannot be a Christian unless one regards the word of the Bible as divinely inspired. Such an attitude would have been regarded as a reactionary even in 1880. Applicants are insulted and trapped—but not so blatantly as in 1916—although even now questions such as "Would you feel happy if you knew our army had all run away?" serve only the purpose of revealing the curious mentality of some of the tribunal members. Again applicants in some cases are led by skilful questioning to the position of showing that they do not believe in fire brigades or compulsory education. No objector, however, who has adequately explored the implications of his position need allow himself to be led into such *impasses* of thought.

One of the serious features of these tribunals is the hostility to political objectors. We have shown (page 19) that conscience can be political. Members of some of the smaller religious sects do not always receive favourable treatment from tribunals, but on the whole a sincere religious objector can expect to receive some form of exemption. Not so the political. In two of these cases taken to the Appellate Tribunal by the Ministry of Labour in December, 1939, the decision of the local tribunal was reversed, apparently on the ground that the applicants did not conscientiously object to all war. It was stated that this decision was not to be regarded as a precedent and some local tribunals have since admitted that a political objection may be conscientious. It is quite likely, however, that the brunt of the struggle for freedom of conscience and liberty will in this war fall on the socialist and political objector.

It is important that religious and ethical objectors should show their solidarity and unity with the political objectors. The latter may not agree that every war is wrong, but at least they can agree that this war is wrong and that a system of society—which persistently produces war is against their conscience and that a new order is necessary. This agreement should be brought out in their statement to the tribunal, the Press and at meetings.

Chairmen of tribunals, Tory Members of Parliament and reactionaries have frequently denounced the efforts of the Peace Pledge Union and other anti-conscription bodies which have organized the holding of test tribunals and assistance to conscientious objectors. They have said that these arrangements undertook to manufacture consciences, and, in the name of freedom, demands have been made that they should be suppressed. Nothing is further from the truth than this accusation. Those who have real experience of the workings of conscience know that it cannot be manufactured at short notice. The purpose of these efforts is to help the young men to elucidate and clear their minds, to make them understand, to show them the positions which are illogical and to explain the procedure at tribunals. Experience of police courts and tribunals shows how formidable it is for a person unskilled in the presentation of a case to state his views openly in public. Is it a manufacture of conscience to explain to a conscientious objector that his statement that war is murder is not accurate? Murder is a peculiar and technical legal definition and it does not make for clear thinking to apply it to the mass slaughter of human beings which modern war involves.

Behind the conscientious objectors of 1939-40 there has not been perhaps the same unity, fellowship and drive as there was in 1915-18. Conscientious objectors have been too apt to think only of their own conscience and not to relate it sufficiently to the general questions of conscription, freedom and social reconstruction. There is too often lack of thought and knowledge. A conscientious objector has even been met with who stated that he had a conscience against taking part in war but no reasons for it!!

On the conscientious objector at this moment particularly depends the survival of the principle of freedom of conscience and freedom of expression of opinion—that the two are inseparable and stand or fall together. It is impossible for a conscientious objector to read, study and think too much about the problems of pacifism, conscience and freedom. If he is to fulfil his social obligations he must understand the reason why he is a conscientious objector, the necessary implications of his stand and the necessity for practical work. Too many conscientious objectors when they have been before a tribunal accept the decision and enter into no effective relation with the conscientious objectors' movement thereafter. Their conscience is not sufficiently educated.

Moreover, the objector to war who does not go on to advocate the reconstruction of society has a very limited and narrow conscience. If his conscience takes no account of the poverty and misery of most of the population, and if he does not regard some fundamental change as necessary, then indeed he needs educating.

Conscription in 1939 found this movement in a very different position from 1916 but at first there was no proper co-ordination. There have been cases of conscientious objectors who have passed through tribunals and have not been contacted by any of the bodies which exist to help them. The work of the Central Board for Conscientious Objectors, 6, Endsleigh Street, W.C.1, and the Fellowship of Conscientious Objectors, 1, Paper Buildings, E.C.4. has brought this to an end. The membership of the Fellowship is now some one thousand five hundred, and it may rise to well over forty thousand. Its objects are to stimulate and encourage the spirit of fellowship between conscientious objectors, to provide a means for such fellowship and to promote understanding and co-operation between peoples in an endeavour to break down the barriers that make them the victims of periodical conflicts. Great is their responsibility.

There is a further difficulty which arises between those who accept alternative service and those who maintain the absolute position. "Alternativists" in particular have to be careful to avoid a lack of understanding of, and sympathy for, the absolutist. Those who are willing to accept non-combatant service in the armed forces or to accept civilian work under civilian control are in particular danger of being disparate and unconscious of the fact that they are part of a wider movement.

We are glad to record that Great Britain showed in the 1914 war and in this war is showing more recognition of the principles of freedom of conscience than any other belligerent. In America in 1917–18 the Conscience Clause was much narrower than here, and in France a conscientious objector has never been recognized. The Government has stated that the conscientious objectors of the past have taught them that you cannot force men to fight against their convictions, and as further proof of their earnestness they have set up an advisory tribunal to whom conscientious objectors in the armed forces can apply, if they are undergoing imprison-

ment imposed by a court-martial, and if they are persons wh
did not originally register as conscientious objectors. There is n
reason to doubt the present sincerity of the Government. Muck
however, depends on public opinion, and lately there have bee
expressions of violent feeling against the pacifist and the con
scientious objector. There are increasing demands for their dis
missal. The working class who gained some of the freedom—
limited though it is—which until recently they enjoyed throug
the predecessors of the conscientious objectors, now turn on thos
who at present uphold the cause, and in some cases demand thei
dismissal—enforcing their demand by strike action. Many loca
authorities and employers of labour have dismissed all thei
conscientious objectors for the duration of the war. These action
are always accompanied by high sounding phrases such a
"equality of sacrifice" but the intention is to penalize men wh
dare to differ from the majority. Local tribunals are showin
their prejudice increasingly and are more and more denying t
genuine conscientious objectors the exemption to which they ar
entitled.

Words like "conscience," "liberty" and "freedom" are con
stantly bandied about in England and the emotional attachment
of the words confuse their users and prevent them from under
standing the principles which lie—or should lie behind. Ye
freedom of conscience and freedom of thought will only b
secure when the principles which make these necessary for an
State fit to live in, are understood and accepted.

One of the important tasks of the conscientious objector i
to understand and think out his principles himself and throug
his organizations to strengthen their practice. For as the wa
continues and hate and the desire for revenge increase, suc
attachment as the majority has to these principles may be easil
swept away in a gust of war fever, prejudice and emotion
despite the good intentions of the Government. Under the power
conferred by the Emergency Powers (Defence) Act, 1940, th
Conscience Clause in the National Service (Armed Forces) Ac

can be overridden. Any person can be conscripted for military or industrial purposes. It is not necessarily expected that these powers will be used to their full extent, but this possibility must be envisaged. The Minister of Labour has, at present, been given power to direct any person to perform any service at the rate of pay and on conditions of services to be settled by the Minister. There is no Conscience Clause. All honest lovers of freedom must wish the genuine conscientious objector to stand firm.

Whither are we tending?

Is it to the bureaucratic State, perhaps even to totalitarianism? What must be the future policy of the defenders of freedom of conscience, and liberty of opinion? To this we now turn.

Chapter 9

WHAT OF THE FUTURE?

Courage yet, my brother or my sister!
Keep on—Liberty is to be subserv'd whatever occurs;
That is nothing that is quell'd by one or two failures, or any
*   number of failures,*
Or by the indifference or ingratitude of the people, or by any
*   unfaithfulness,*
Or the show of the tushes of power, soldiers, cannon, penal
*   statutes.*

What we believe in waits latent forever through all the
*   continents,*
Invites no one, promises nothing, sits in calmness and light,
*   is positive and composed, knows no discouragement,*
Waiting patiently, waiting its time.

WALT WHITMAN.

"The true revolution will be that which putting conscience above all other mundane considerations—will abolish in politics and in all social relations the frightful principle of *raison-d'état,* which under the pretext of order, honour, public welfare, or morals, sometimes allows one to commit oneself and sometimes excuses in others the most evident and patent crimes."[1] The truth of this saying is surely only too plain to-day. It has been shown in this book that freedom of conscience and liberty of opinion are necessary and desirable. They are founded firmly on the premise of the value of the individual. The belief that the individual is the ultimate value and that State activity only

[1] Quoted from Proudhon by Alfred Cobban

exists to promote his well-being and happiness has had a long and chequered history. From time to time emerging into the daylight of widespread acceptance, it has, as we have shown, again been crushed by Emperors, Churches, parliaments and barons, landlords, kings, dictators and other ruling persons and groups. As Leonard Woolf points out in *After the Deluge*,[1] the ordinary man living in the eighteenth century would have been astonished at the suggestion that he was of equal value with the man who governed him, but the wide diffusion of this belief in the individual had already begun; as a result of the reformation and the various religious bodies which it led to, men were beginning to practise governing themselves. The establishment of the Society of Friends based on the principle that every man had something of God within him and was of equal value in the sight of God led to the view that nothing must be done to injure or impair an individuality. Voltaire, influenced by Quaker and other thought, spread this principle during the eighteenth century. The American Rebellion and the French Revolution gave further impetus to ideas of democracy and personal liberty. What do these expressions mean to those who use them to-day? Leonard Woolf's definition of democracy is as clear as any: "(1) every class within the community has politically the same right to happiness as every other class and every individual the same right to happiness as every other individual; (2) the equality of the citizens consists primarily in their equal rights to liberty and happiness and secondarily in their right to equality before the law." But all this is based finally on the belief that every individual is of equal value, and has an equal right to happiness, although, of course, this does not mean that every individual has equal capacity.

Some of the early democrats imagined that when they had attained political democracy and had abolished political privileges, the millennium would dawn: but they were to be disillusioned. They discovered that the privilege of property remained to be

[1] Pelican Series (A 18), 6d.

dealt with, and that this was a great obstacle in the way of attaining that equality which is necessary if the right of every individual to be treated as a separate unit in society and politically and socially of equal value is to be secured. The development of nationalism, too, obscured and confused the growing recognition of the needs of the individual. This is not the place to enter into an examination of the causes for the rise of nationalism.[1] For our purposes only its later stages are of interest. Recently it has become only too clear that ideas of democracy and nationalism fused together but unleavened by a sense of the value of individual liberty develop a narrow destructive energy that bids fair to ruin civilization altogether. To-day the idea of the value of the individual is threatened as it never has been before for the last two hundred years. It is denied both in theory and in practice by the totalitarian, police and dictator states. In England and America it has lip service paid to it, but even in these countries the growth of the military power, the increasing militarism of the police force, and the new bureaucracy threaten it increasingly. It is, therefore, pertinent to enquire what should be done to preserve this principle and to defend and extend the principles of liberty and freedom of conscience. It is first of all imperative that men should be clear as to what they believe in and why they believe it. There is much thoughtless acceptance of confused ideas; men must understand, as Leonard Woolf says, "that the State is to be regarded from the point of view of civilization as on the same level as a drainage system or a power station. It has no more connection with our best selves than has a sewage farm, and it is reasonable to expect just as little and just as much sweetness and light in the State as in a water closet. . . . It will have the same amount of culture and reason as have the individuals who compose or control it," and indeed its action very often indicates that it has much less.

[1] For further discussion of the problems of nationalism and dictatorship see *Dictatorship, Its History and Theory*, by Alfred Cobban (Jonathan Cape, 1939).

The next step is to realize that liberty and freedom of conscience can only be preserved and developed within a democracy. In the past it has too often been assumed that democracy implied liberty. It had sometimes been believed that the will of the majority was almost divine, and that with universal suffrage there would be automatic progress towards Utopia. It is now realized that this is by no means the case, and the emphasis should perhaps to-day be thrown on the freedom of the individual conscience and liberty rather than on democracy; nevertheless to make these secure the machinery of democracy must also be there and in working order.

Political democracy is not yet complete in England. The House of Lords still remains a body of vested interests ready to block and delay the measures of any progressive government. The only second Chamber which is tolerable to healthy democracy is one like the Norwegian Chamber where party membership is in the same proportion as the Lower House which elects it. It has useful powers of revision but not of delay.

The method of election to the British House of Commons itself needs revision. The present system does not ensure that the House of Commons represents the nation. In 1919 the Government with 5,101,000 votes obtained 472 seats, and although the opposition had 4,674,000 votes they only obtained 136. The result was that there was not adequate opposition to or criticism of the Treaty of Versailles. If such opinion in the country as was in favour of moderation and reason had been properly represented in Parliament, there might well have been a fairer Peace Treaty and no second war against Germany.

The case for the adoption of proportional representation[1] is overwhelming, and the only reason why change is delayed is that political parties think they benefit from the present system. Note, for instance, that in 1924 the Conservative Party obtained a majority of 176 seats in Parliament although the total opposition vote was over one million more than the Tory vote. This system

[1] See the publications of the P.R. Society, 82 Victoria Street, S.W.1.

of election—P.R.—has worked exceedingly well in the Irish Free State and was only abolished in Northern Ireland because it gave the minorities a fair representation. It has been adopted by New York and other large American towns for local elections, and is successfully in operation in other parts of the British Empire and elsewhere.

It is clearly a system which should be applied to our local elections. In London there are Metropolitan boroughs without a single Labour representative or a single Conservative member, notwithstanding large numbers of electors who voted for the opposition. The existence of large sections of unrepresented opinion tends to destroy confidence in democracy and the system of government (local or central) by representation.

The procedure of the House of Commons has for many years been regarded as archaic and designed not to facilitate legislation but to obstruct it. The latest proposals for reform are those put forward in Sir Stafford Cripps's *Democracy Up to Date*.[1]

The question of the control of rules, regulations and orders issued by government departments has already been dealt with (see Chapter 6), but the reader may be reminded that this is an essential part of democracy. Every law must have the consent of the people. At present government departments make new rules with practically no control, and if democracy is to be effective the House of Commons must control them.

Sir Stafford Cripps suggests that advisory committees should be set up to be attached to each government department. These committees would have the advantage of being able to utilize the services of private members. They would be able to assist and advise the Minister of the department concerned; calls for information and reports and details of bills could be dealt with by them. Moreover, every rule, order and regulation would have to be submitted to them. It is not suggested that these committees should be executive bodies as in the case of local authorities. They would mainly be advisory. The experience of local autho-

[1] George Allen & Unwin, 2s.

rities has shown how valuable it is for all their members to be attached to some work of administration. Moreover, the constant contact of members with Ministers would tend to make Ministers more responsible, and bureaucracy could not be so irresponsible. The average private member in the House of Commons is so much a mere cog in the party machine that one wonders sometimes why people are so anxious to be able to add "M.P." to their names. This reform would give to the House of Commons some of its former influence and would ensure that control over the Government which is so urgently necessary.

A form of procedure which would assist private members' bills is also suggested by Sir Stafford Cripps. Many bills which urgently need enacting make no progress because they are not comprised in some party programme, or because they cut across party lines. The Royal Commission on divorce reported in favour of Divorce Law Reform in 1912, but although there is no doubt that the vast majority of people in the country were in favour of the proposed reforms, nothing was done until 1937 when Mr. A. P. Herbert secured the enactment of the majority of the recommendations. It is intolerable that reforms like this, or like that contained in The Access to Mountains Act, 1939, which took even longer to enact, should be held up for a generation or more, and in the meantime millions of lives are unhappier as a result. Technical reforms of the law are also delayed because they would not add to any party's number of votes at the next general election. That at any rate is how the parties view such proposals, but a truly imaginative policy would know how to popularize them.

There does not seem to be any reason why debates in the House of Commons should not be confined to questions of principle. It is obviously ridiculous to consider long and complicated bills line by line in the Committee of the whole House. Why should there be two debates of principle on every bill, so that what is said on the second reading is repeated again, with exactly the same argument on the third reading? Devices like this, and the absence of devices for mechanical voting, seem to be designed to waste time: indeed the whole procedure and standing orders of the House of Commons appear sometimes to be a hundred years out of date.

The public's ignorance of much of the work of the civil service, and the lack of contact which the civil service has with lay opinion, was commented on by the Machinery of Government Committee in 1918.[1] They made the important suggestion that there should be attached to each department an advisory committee of citizens who are particularly affected by the work of that department as, for example, the work of the Consultative Committee of the Board of Education. Such a committee attached to the Ministry of Labour might have taught the officials responsible for its policy much about the administration of the means test, and conditions in the distressed areas. Moreover the adoption of this proposal would greatly help to educate the public in the workings of the constitution and the way that the laws are administered.

Democratic control of foreign affairs and policy has still to be achieved. It was much discussed during the last war, but despite one or two efforts by Labour Governments, there has been little or no change. Secret treaties, despite the Covenant of the League of Nations, can still be made without the knowledge or consent of Parliament. The House of Commons is always presented with an accomplished fact, the rejection of which would involve the downfall of the Government and a general election, except in cases where there has been an unauthorized leakage (e.g. the Hoare-Laval incident). There seems much to be said for a law providing that no treaty shall be valid without the consent of the House of Commons. A similar provision has been found useful in America and would help to keep the public informed and interested in foreign affairs. The League of Nations Covenant was never made an Act of Parliament and many conventions of the International Labour Office were never even

[1] Cd. 9230.

brought before Parliament, despite the mandatory provisions of the Treaty of Versailles. Such a state of affairs must not be allowed to recur.

Political democracy does not only depend on a democratic central government. A vital and deep interest in local government is one of the most important functions of a democratic people. It has for many generations been one of the safeguards of English political democracy that so many men and women of good calibre have been willing to serve the community in a voluntary capacity on local authorities all over the country. Often they get little or no public or widespread recognition of their work. Yet it is indispensable.[1]

The necessity for the reform of the election of local authorities has already been mentioned. Attention should also be called to the necessity for releasing them from the need of having to apply to Parliament whenever they want additional powers, such as being able to run a theatre or a bank. There is need for much reform in this field.

The petty jealousies of local authorities with each other often prevent some service, such as education or health, being properly developed. For certain services, such as gas, electricity and certain others, it is probable that Regional Authorities will have to be established. In London local government is still based on a plan adopted as long ago as 1888. The confusion and welter of authorities[2] for greater London is perhaps greater than anywhere else.

The vitality of democracy does not, however, consist only in central and local governments. Voluntary associations of all kinds form an essential part. Besides the political parties and the trade unions, which have existed for many years, democracy shows its continued vitality in throwing up new forms of associ-

[1] See e.g. *The Development of Local Government*, by W. A. Robson. (George Allen & Unwin).

[2] See *The Government and Mis-Government of London*, by W. A. Robson.

ation as new needs develop. Societies for cultural purposes and sport have always flourished in some degree, but recent years have seen the development of tenants defence leagues which in some districts have secured reduction in rents amounting to thousands of pounds per annum. These bodies tend, as they develop, to concern themselves with the general interests of their members in all aspects of public life. Left Book Club groups and Peace Pledge Union groups are active not only for the purpose for which they were started, but in local matters and for general social problems. Before the war one of the most interesting developments on these lines was the growth of community centres, not only on new housing estates but in crowded areas. These are often due to the initiative of the local authority, but are run by a committee representing the members. If these could only be more freely and fully developed they would go far to remedy the helpless superficiality of English social life. A tribute must be paid to the Peckham Health Centre for its pioneer work in associating health with such a communal centre. Since the war other organizations have developed, amongst them A.R.P. posts, associations of distressed traders and manufacturers: all these associations and the older ones are potential centres of resistance against tyranny, but to make them effective in this regard they must have some members who understand the importance of principle. The effect of the war will be to make the existence of minority societies much more difficult. They have already been severely handicapped by the heavy increase in postage charges and as taxation increases and their subscribers have less and less money to spare so will their existence be more and more imperilled. It is now an imperative duty of the progressive to support minority societies and movements, and also progressive papers and periodicals to the utmost of his financial ability.

To secure liberty more firmly the whole machinery of justice needs to be drastically overhauled. A Government committee at the end of the 1914 war recommended that a Ministry of Justice should be set up. It would be one of the tasks of this ministry to be responsible for and to promote law reform—a task at present undertaken by no Government department. The most urgent reform necessary in the system of the Courts is the reform of the Police Courts or Courts of Summary Jurisdiction. The practice of appointing magistrates for political reasons should cease. The Howard League for Penal Reform has made a suggestion that Inspectors should visit Magistrates' Courts not to enforce law but to advise them. This would result in the removal of many of the cases of gross injustice which at present so often occur. There is a need for the democratization of the police force, and an end should be put to the practice of appointing retired military officers to be chief constables. The whole personnel of the Courts needs to be reviewed but until society ceases to have class distinctions it will not be possible to do all that is necessary. Proposals for the reform of legal education have been made from time to time during the last forty years but so far have been little acted upon. Yet the lawyers and law courts have a special function to play in defending liberty, and the need of a broader and more enlightened education is imperative. These proposed changes lead us to the related questions of prison reform and punishment, all of which bear on this question of liberty. But here we must be content with remarking that the passage into law of the Criminal Justice Bill, 1939, would have removed many blots from the English penal system.

The problem of the B.B.C. may be mentioned here. It has consistently refused to allow the expression of opinion through the microphone to small minorities. Rationalists, Communists, Spiritualists have all been banned. Well-known speakers have had their speeches censored and an intolerable attitude towards its employee's private lives has been shown (all employees who were divorced were at one time dismissed). To remedy this state of things and to promote a healthy competition the suggestion that autonomous broadcasting corporations should be set up for Wales, Scotland and the various regions of England should be very carefully considered. The monopoly of the B.B.C. would be effectively destroyed in this wap.

It has been stated before—and it cannot be too strongly emphasized—that liberty and democracy will never be secure until there is economic equality—so long as most of the wealth of the nation and its income are owned by a few the majority are doomed to poverty, mal-nutrition, bad housing and depressing lives. The value of the individual is disregarded, and liberty and democracy are assumed to be the privileges of the few. The democrat must realize this and work for social change. This is no place to go into details as to how the change must be secured, or as to the nature of economic equality. Call it Socialism, call it the Co-operative Commonwealth, what you will; it is necessary that political liberty and democracy shall be used to attain it or inequality will destroy liberty. This has been the lesson of events in Germany, Italy and other countries. It is perhaps the most difficult problem which faces democrats here—how to make the necessary change quickly and peacefully. This book is concerned to emphasize that any change which is made will not be for the better if the principles of liberty and democracy are ignored, or forgotten.

What further steps must be taken to safeguard liberty? The proper education of children in these principles is one of the most important. To educate men to be rational; to train them for citizenship and to inculcate the principles of liberty and democracy; these are the problems. As to how this is to be done the experts must decide, but the aim must be that those who have been educated should accept the necessity for liberty, freedom and democracy as naturally as the majority now accept the ideas of patriotism, and that of death at the will of the State. Fascist governments have shown how education in intolerance can succeed. Much of their method is neutral and can be equally well employed for the inculcation of a love of tolerance and freedom. Mr. Cobban suggests in *Dictatorship, Its History and Theory* that the increasing trend towards specialization in education is making it more difficult for men to understand the art of government and the necessity for ethical values, and he suggests that this trend in education is strictly relevant to the rise of dictatorship. As he says: "Unguarded either by belief in an ancient creed or by a rational study of the problems of social life, the expert is ready to fall a victim to any new heresy. He will seize on any gospel that has the appearance of providing a safe orthodoxy on which to base the crumbling state, so long as it is presented by demagogues sufficiently clever or by tyrants sufficiently powerful."

What further steps can be taken? Professor Laski has suggested that a Bill of Rights declaring fundamental liberties is useful, and he instances America where liberty as enacted in the Constitution is taught to all children and with this early inculcation of principle it is thus made easier to resist any encroachment upon it. The average man is said to understand more easily what is being attacked. In England liberties are not safeguarded by any Act of Parliament and must be collected from numerous acts and from decisions of the law courts. It may however be urged against the proposals of Professor Laski that, if liberties are all gathered together in a written document, it is easier for those who wish to attack them to get rid of them by suspending that statute. It is said that if liberty is not legally defined, it is more easily defended. It is not clear whether this is the verdict of the experience of the last twenty years, although it is very clear indeed that the written guarantees of liberty in Germany and elsewhere have been no safeguard. There is, however, a widespread movement for the adoption all over the world of an up-to-date edition of the *Rights of Man*. This movement was originally set on foot by Mr. H. G. Wells,[1] who has contributed so much to the free discussion of this century's problems.

The first document as drafted by him has been revised[2] and a

---

[1] See *Rights of Man*, by H. G. Wells (Penguin Special, 6d.).
[2] See *The Common Sense of Peace and War*, by H. G. Wells (Penguin Special, 6d.).

movement is on foot to press for its adoption by every democratic and liberal-minded party, society, movement and country.

It should be mentioned that the 1940 edition of these Rights of Man represents only a minimum standard. Some English laws are in advance of them. I would suggest that in England the defenders of liberty and democracy might well draft a charter of liberty: this might start in the first place with Mr. H. G. Wells's *Rights of Man*, continue with a statement of the more specific English liberties, and finally conclude by a schedule of every Act of Parliament, rule, order and regulation which is inconsistent with these principles and demanding their repeal and abrogation. At the same time steps might be taken to curb the new bureaucracy and to reform Parliament as before suggested. To take this offensive would undoubtedly help the defence of liberty and democracy, and hearten their defenders. For twenty years or more we have been on the defensive and losing slowly. Liberty is never static and it is time to lose the defensive mentality.

On the conscientious objector of to-day depends in particular the defence of freedom of conscience, liberty of opinion and democracy. His claim, to sum up, is this: "The State has no universal or supreme jurisdiction; nor would an unthinking and uncritical obedience be any real service to the body politic itself. We shall not resist by reason of political disagreement or disapproval, or because we question the wisdom of a method adopted, still less from any feeling aroused by the threat of personal loss of position and privilege. Not for purposes of propaganda, that the cause may have attention drawn to it, will such refusal be right: but only when to refuse is an inescapable duty to a higher authority. Then, after weighty pondering of the issue and inward wrestling as to the truth of our claim and the reality of our guidance, we shall refuse compliance, separate ourselves, it may be, from the majority of our fellows, and seek to stand firm in that resistance. A responsible moral being has a power of judgment, a conscience, a standard, an ideal of how life should be lived. These are his distinctive human attributes, and they cannot be denied or betrayed without descending to a lower level and weakening the very spring of his being. He cannot cast the responsibility upon anyone else, neither Government nor the action of another country, nor a commanding officer. He makes his own decision. Indeed, the crucial question when it does become his duty to refuse obedience is a very individual matter: it is difficult to answer in general terms. Everyone must find out for himself the place where obedience to the law would mean treachery to the paramount claims of conscience."[1]

We have shown that indissolubly linked with the freedom of conscience is the question of liberty of opinion and action. Against the tyranny of the State the conscientious objector stands for the right to act on what his conscience says and for the right to tell his fellow citizens the result of his conscientious thinking and to ask them to examine and educate their own consciences. Other organizations such as the National Council for Civil Liberties may do the detailed work of defending and extending liberty, but if the conscientious objector is to be really successful he must work in the closest possible association with them and realize that he stands for democracy and liberty, as well as a free conscience, and this particular responsibility of those between 18 and 41 may well be shared by other sections of the community.

If this war lasts, as it well may, for several years, there are powers to conscript persons of all ages and sexes for military, industrial and agricultural purposes to assist the war. It is said that conscription is even to be continued after the war and this struggle for freedom of conscience and liberty may well last the rest of this generation.

The responsibility is the responsibility of every individual. Changes can only be initiated by individuals or small groups. Ruggiero[2] says: "Without freedom, religious faith degenerates

[1] *Report of Commission II to the Friends World Conference, 1937* ("The Individual and the State")

[2] *History of European Liberalism*, by G. de Ruggiero (Clarendon Press, Oxford).

into a paralysis and servile submission; science congeals into dogma; art shrivels into imitation; the production of economic wealth declines; and the life of human society sinks to the level of animal society. Freedom is an expansive force, differentiating itself and propagating itself in its effects, to each of which it gives a tone of novelty and originality, which is the tone of the spirit, the distinctive mark of the individual."

This freedom is the freedom of conscience, freedom of liberty, of opinion and the freedom of democracy. These three liberties cannot be separated and in the end they stand or fall together. To show this, to hearten their defenders and to help their diffusion, has been the aim of this essay.

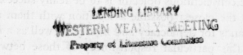
118

Suggestions for further Reading

Liberty in the Modern State, by Professor H. J. Laski (Pelican Series, 6d.).

On Liberty, by John Stuart Mill (Thinker's Library, Watts & Co., 1s. 3d.)

Report of the Royal Commission on Police Powers and Procedure (1929, Cmd. 3297, Stationery Office, 3s.).

Liberty To-day, by C. E. M. Joad (Thinker's Library, 1s. 3d.).

Report of the Crown Proceedings Committee (1927, Cmd. 2842, Stationery Office, 9d.).

Penalties upon Opinion, by H. Bradlaugh Bonner (Thinker's Library, 1s. 3d.).

The Press, by Wickham Steed (Penguin Special, 6d.).

The Banned Books of England, by Alec Craig (George Allen & Unwin, 7s. 6d.).

Report of the Commission on Ministers' Powers (1932, Cmd. 4060, Stationery Office, 2s. 6d.).

The Struggle for the Freedom of the Press, 1819–32, by William Wickwar (George Allen & Unwin, 7s. 6d.).

Departmental Commission on the Imposition of Penalties by Marketing Boards and Similar Bodies (Cmd. 5980, Stationery Office, 1s.).

Thinking to Some Purpose, by Susan Stebbings (Pelican, 6d.).

War and Human Values, by F. E. Pollard. (*Out of print.*)

A History of Freedom of Thought, by J. B. Bury (Home University Library, 2s. 6d.).

Historical Trials, by Sir John MacDonell (Clarendon Press, Oxford, and Watts & Co., 1s. 3d.).

The Quakers in Peace and War, by M. E. Hirst (George Allen & Unwin, 3s. 6d.).

Conscription and Conscience, by J. W. Graham (George Allen & Unwin). (*Out of print.*)

Civil Liberties, W. H. Thompson (Victor Gollancz, 1s.).

Food in War Time (The Fabian Society, 2d.).

Bureaucracy Run Mad, by Martin Abbotson (Watts & Co., 1s. 3d.).

After the Deluge, by Leonard Woolf (The Hogarth Press and Pelican Series, 6d.).

Dictatorship, Its History and Theory, by Alfred Cobban (Jonathan Cape Ltd.).

Democracy Up to Date, by Sir Stafford Cripps (George Allen & Unwin, 2s.).

Development of Local Government, by W. A. Robson (George Allen & Unwin, 12s. 6d.).

Government and Mis-Government of London, by W. A. Robson (George Allen & Unwin).

Rights of Man, by H. G. Wells (Penguin Special, 6d.).

A History of European Liberalism, by G. de Ruggiero (Clarendon Press, Oxford).

Power, by Bertrand Russell (George Allen & Unwin, 7s. 6d.).

The New Despotism, by Lord Hewart (Ernest Benn Ltd., 5s.).

Report of the Machinery of Government Committee (Cmd. 9230, Stationery Office).

Report of Commission II to the Friends World Conference, 1937 ("The Individual and the State"). (Friends' Bookshop).

Civilization and Liberty, by Ramsey Muir (Jonathan Cape, 2s. 6d.).

The Common Sense of War and Peace, by H. G. Wells (Penguin Special, 6d.).

Why Freedom Matters, by Sir Norman Angel (Penguin Special, 6d.).

British Liberty in Danger, by Ronald Kidd, Secretary N.C.C.L. (Lawrence & Wishart, 5s.).

Can Conscience be Measured, by Reginald A. Smith (Bloomsbury Publishing Co., 1s. 6d.).

Troublesome People (Control Board for C.O's., 1s.).

Justice and Liberty, by G. Lowes Dickinson (George Allen & Unwin, 6s.).

The Fourth Protocol of Political Liberty, Selected by Ernest Rhys (Dent's Everyman Library, 2s.).

Index

Absolutist objector, 97, 101

Access to Mountains Act, 109

Acts of Indemnity, 46

Affirmation Bill (Bradlaugh's), 46

Agricultural Marketing Act, 1933, 77

Allen, Clifford, 67

Alternativist Objector, 101

American Rebellion, 105

American War of Independence, 40

Arrest, power of, 90

Bacon, Roger, 34

B.B.C.—
  attitude to employees, 113
  censorship, 113
  monopoly, 114
  reform of, 113–14.

Bill of Rights, 115

Birkenhead, Lord, 59

Blasphemous libel, 44, 45

Blasphemy Act, 1698, 45

Blasphemy laws, 24, 48, 74

Blasphemy, penalties for, 45

Bradlaugh, 45, 46

Bruno, 36

Bureaucracy, 75, 92, 93, 94, 106, 116

Burke, 51

Calvin, 35

Carlile, Richard, 44

Casement, Roger, 59

Catholic education prohibition of, 47

Cecil, Lord Hugh, 68

Censorship, 52, 90

Chief of Police—
  appointment of, 113
  power of, 89

Christianity, 22, 33, 55

Civil Liberties, National Council of, 52, 58, 69, 117

Conscience, 11, 61
  authority of, 17–18
  as divine intervention, 12
  as function of mind, 12
  clause (American), 101
  compulsion of, 29
  development of, 16
  education of, 18
  elements of, 12, 13
  freedom of, 18, 28, 35, 51, 62, 63, 67, 100, 101, 102, 103, 104, 106, 116, 117, 118
  future of, 15
  infallibility of, 17
  nature of, 11
  primitive, 15
  recognition in law, 11
  rights of, 40

Conscientious objection to war, 13

Conscientious objector, 30, 97, 101, 117

Conscientious objectors—
  as non-combatants, 41
  Central Board for, 101
  court-martialled, 64
  death penalty for, 62

Conscientious objectors
(*contd.*)—
  denied unemployment bene-
    fit, 81
  deprived of vote, 68
  dismissal of, 102
  exemption from military ser-
    vice, 62
  Fellowship of, 101
  in military prisons, 66
  lack of unity among, 100
  military treatment of, 65, 66
  persecution of, 41
  registering of, 95
  sentenced to death, 64
Conscription, 62, 95, 101, 117
Conscription Acts, 1914–18, 11
Constantine, Emperor, 33
Corruption of Public Morale, 88
Court martial, trial of civilians,
    59, 84
Courts of referees, representa-
    tion before, 80
Criminal Justice Bill, 1939, 113
Cripps, Sir Stafford, 78, 108,
    109
Crown Proceedings Bill, 82

Death Penalty, 91
Defence of Realm Acts, 51, 52,
    59, 60, 84, 85
Defence Regulations, 43, 85
Democracy, 28, 106, 107, 111
Detention—
  power of, 85, 86
  without trial, 84
Dictatorship, 56
Divorce Law Reform, 109
Donoughmore Committee, 76,
    77

Economic equality, 114

Education, 114
Election reform, 111
Emergency Powers Act, 1920, 69
Emergency Powers (Defence)
    Act, 1939, 43, 83, 85, 91,
    92, 93
Emergency Powers (Defence)
    Act, 1940, 84, 102
Emergency Powers (Defence)
    Acts, provisions for death
    penalty, 84
Ethical objectors, 99

Fisher, Rt. Hon. H. A. L., 97
Fleming, Lord, 97
Food Controllers, 92
Fox, George, 36
French Revolution, 44, 105

Galileo, 36
General Strike, 1926, 29, 70
Government Departments—
  no claims against, 81
  powers of, 75–82
Graham, J. W., 62, 65

Habeas Corpus, 60, 61, 69, 77,
    85
Herbert, A. P., 109
Hewart, Lord, 70, 93
House of Commons—
  debates, 109
  election of, 107
  procedure of, 108, 110
House of Lords, reform of, 107

Illegal Literature, search for
    possession of, 58
Incitement to Disaffection Act,
    71, 86
Inquisition, 18, 34
Insulting words and behaviour,
    72

Internment, 60, 85
Irish Coercion Acts, 48

Joan of Arc, 34
Jones, Ernest, 20
Justice, machinery of, 112

Laski, H. J., 27, 56, 115
Law reform, 109, 113
Lawyers, prohibition of, before
    Committees, etc., 80, 94
League of Nations Covenant,
    110
Left Book Club, 112
Legislation, delegated powers of,
    78, 79
Liberty, 20, 28, 30, 69, 92, 118
    American, 115
    diminishing of civil, 82
    history of, 31–103
    principles of, 21
    safeguarding of, 114
    statutory attacks on, 69 *et. seq.*
Literature, illegal possession of,
    88
Lloyd George, 53
Lollards, 36
London Local Government, 111

Machinery of Government Com-
    mittee, 110
Mann, Tom, 73
Marcus Aurelius, 33
Married women and property,
    35
Meetings, prohibition of, 84, 89
Military representative, 63
Military Service Acts, 51, 62, 67,
    96
Military Training Act, 1939, 77,
    78, 95
Mill, John Stuart, 20, 24

Milton, 11, 52
Ministerial Orders, right to
    challenge, 76
Ministers' Powers, Committee
    on, 76
Minority Societies, 112
Moors in Spain, 34
Morris, William, 31
Moslem women, freedom of, 35

National Service (Armed Forces)
    Act, 1939, 87, 95
News, suppression of, 53
No-Conscription Fellowship,
    64, 67
Nonconformists, 46
    acts of suppression for, 37
    liberty of, 48
    religious freedom for, 47

Oath of Supremacy, 47
Oaths of Abjuration, 38
Obscenity laws, 24
Official Secrets Act, 1920, 70
Open-air meetings, police
    powers, 72
Opinion—
    freedom of, 23–30, 61, 103,
        104, 116, 117, 118
    suppression of, 25, 55, 91
Organizations, prohibition of, 90
    right to suppress, 26

Pacifist propaganda, 87
Paine, Thomas, 44
Parliament, delegation of power,
    75
Parmoor, Lord, 60
Peaceful picketing, 71
Peace Pledge Union, 98, 99, 112
Peckham Health Centre, 112
Penn, William, 37

Pennsylvania, 39–40
Persons' movements, control of, 86
Petition of Right, 82
Police Courts, reform of, 113
Political objectors, 99
Pollard, Francis E., 29
Pope Innocent III, 34
Possession of prohibited documents, 54
Price of Goods Act, 1939, 94
Printing machinery, seizure of, 89
Printing, prohibition of, 89
Private meeting, police powers, of entry, 73
Private members' bills, 109
Private property, 28
Propaganda, suppression of, 87
Proportional representation, 107
Public meetings—
    attacks on, 57, 58
    interference with right of, 57, 72
    prohibition of, 57
Public opinion—
    coercive effect of, 24
    mass standardization of, 24
Public Order Act, 1936, 33, 71, 73
Public processions, restrictions on, 71

Quakers—
    in Pennsylvania, 40
    Militia Acts for, 39
    persecution of, 38
    refusal to pay tithes, 47

Rationalist Societies, 48
Reform Bill, 1832, 44
Reformation, 22, 35

Religious freedom, struggle for, 46
Religious liberty, 35
Religious objectors, 99
Rights of Man, 115
Roman Catholic Church, 35, 36
Roman Catholics—
    Act for relief of, 48
    laws against, 47
    liberty of, 48
Roman Empire, 22
Royal Commission on Police Powers, 1929, 42
Ruggiero, G. de, 117
Russell, Bertrand, 25
Russia, 53

Scepticism, need for, 25
Search, power of, 43, 72, 90
Secret Treaties, 110
Sedition, 73
Seditious Meetings Act, 74
Serious Mischief, caused by fomenting opposition to war, 88
Servetus, 35
Shelley, 45
Snowden, Philip, 59
Societies—
    power to dissolve, 84
    State control of, 26
    suppression of, 26, 27
Society of Friends, 36, 39, 54, 55, 63, 105
Socrates, 22, 31
State—
    resistance to, 29
    tyranny of, 117
    view of, 106
Stephen, Sir Leslie, 16
Suffragette movement, 49

Suggestions for reading, 119
Sympathetic strike, 71

Tagore, Rabindranath, 69
Tenants' Defence League, 112
The Tribunal, attempts to suppress, 67
Thomas, J. H., 62
Thompson, W. H., 69, 70
Tiberius, Emperor, 33
Tithes, payment of, 47
Toleration Act, 1689, 37, 46
Toleration Decree, A.D. 311, 33
Trade Disputes and Trade Unions Act, 71
Traders' defence leagues, 112
Treachery Act, 1940, 91
Trials in secret, 93
Tribunals, 19, 62, 63, 64, 93, 96, 97
Tribunals, administrative, 79, 80
Tribunals, appellate, 95, 97, 99

Trophy money, 39

Unemployment Assistance Act, 1934, 80
Unlawful assembly, 74

Vaccination, conscientious objection to, 11
Versailles—
  Peace of, 56
  Treaty of, 107, 111
Virginia Yearly Meeting, memorial of, 40
Voltaire, 105

War, political objection to, 19
Warrants for search of premises, 42, 43
Watson, Dr. Robert Spence, 49
Wells, H. G., 115, 116
Whitman, Walt, 83, 104
Wilkes, 42
Wilkinson, Ellen, 94
Woolf, Leonard, 105, 106

GEORGE ALLEN & UNWIN LTD
LONDON: 40 MUSEUM STREET, W.C.1
CAPE TOWN: 73 ST. GEORGE'S STREET
TORONTO: 91 WELLINGTON STREET WEST
BOMBAY: 15 GRAHAM ROAD, BALLARD ESTATE
WELLINGTON, N.Z.: 8 KINGS CRESCENT, LOWER HUTT
SYDNEY, N.S.W.: AUSTRALIA HOUSE, WYNYARD SQUARE

SEX AND REVOLUTION
by Alec Craig   Cr. 8vo. 4s. 6d.

"Summarizes very sensibly and acutely what most people under thirty, who have given any thought to the matter at all think about sexual relations "—*New English Weekly*

THE BANNED BOOKS OF ENGLAND
by Alec Craig   La. Cr. 8vo. 7s. 6d.

"He does not get excited; he keeps his head; he has examined the law on the subject, and he sets it down clearly with copious examples. . . . He is clear, full, sensible, moderate and compelling."—*The Spectator*

DEMOCRACY UP-TO-DATE
by Sir Stafford Cripps   Cr. 8vo. 2s.

"His arguments for reform are extremely interesting and there can be little doubt that development on the lines suggested by him is desirable."—LEONARD WOOLF in *The Political Quarterly*

MANIFESTO
The Book of the Federation of Progressive Societies and Individuals by C. E. M. Joad, Francis Meynell, W. Olaf Stapledon and others. Introduction by H. G. Wells.

                                                 La. Cr. 8vo. 7s. 6d.

"A document, the interest and importance of which will be recognized even by those who have little sympathy with its point of view."—*John o'London's Weekly*

The address of the F.P.S.I. is now 49 Nassington Road, N.W.3.

RELIGION, MORALS AND INTELLECT
by F. E. Pollard   Cr. 8vo. 5s.

"A vigorous plea for reason as a guide to truth."—*Expository Times*